T0278395

"A journalist, a businessperson, and a minister, Cleghorn has produced a clarion call to the faith community. In *Building Belonging*, he gives us a thoughtful primer on the roots and depth of the housing crisis—in Charlotte and nationwide. He doesn't just analyze the problem but also opens a door for many families of faith to follow God's teachings and share our assets with those in need."
—Hugh McColl, civic leader and former Chairman and Chief Executive Officer, Bank of America Corp.

"*Building Belonging* is like a tall glass of iced lemonade for the parched souls who long to see the church love their neighbors in practical and life-giving ways. John Cleghorn tells the story of how one church wrestled with, and ultimately overcame, the many obstacles that inevitably come from following where Christ leads. This book will inspire many—will inspire you!—to see how God might be calling you and your community to align your resources so that all those whom God loves—which is everyone!—might flourish."
—Jacqueline E. Lapsley, President and Professor of Old Testament, Union Presbyterian Seminary

"The shape of congregational ministry and the use of church buildings and land is shifting radically. Cleghorn's *Building Belonging* offers an inspiring vision of how affordable housing development and church partnerships can come together to create deep community and new possibilities. This book is a must-read for any congregation or leader considering church-based affordable housing!"
—Mark Elsdon, editor of *Gone for Good? Negotiating the Coming Wave of Church Property Transition*

"Cleghorn has delivered us a work that is well researched but even more well lived. The stories of Easter's Home and the dozens more church projects creating affordable housing across the country are a beacon of hope for the American church in a moment of uncertainty. This book offers a road map through the most Christian decision of all—to choose a type of death that brings new life over a form of survival that brings death. This book is urgent, essential, and not a moment too soon."
—Kevin Nye, Housing and Homelessness Director, advocate, and author of *Grace Can Lead Us Home: A Christian Call to End Homelessness*

"You'll find several things in this book: practical steps, theological reflection, case studies of ministry in practice. But at its heart, in my reading, is an essential question about conversion. Cleghorn wants American Christians to examine 'what have we forgotten? And whom have we forgotten?' In our cities and towns, he shows us, we've often forgotten that conversion happens not only in our hearts but in our geography. Faithful Christianity remembers to risk new dreams for our buildings, on our campuses, and in our neighborhoods for the life of the world. *Building Belonging* constructs a vibrant vision of redemptive churches in flourishing cities."

—Greg Jarrell, author of *Our Trespasses: White Churches and the Taking of American Neighborhoods*

"*Building Belonging* is a book of possibility and promise. Readers will walk away from Cleghorn's book looking at their church, their church's property, and their church's community anew. Inspiring God's people to think creatively and act faithfully, Cleghorn has provided a road map for congregations ready to reimagine the use of their property to meet the needs of their neighbors."

—Teri McDowell Ott, editor/publisher of *The Presbyterian Outlook*

"'Churches have to reinvent themselves' is a quote from *Building Belonging*. It is an apt description for the vision inside this book and a call for congregations throughout the nation to utilize their primary resource, the church building, to build the Beloved Community. In a wonderful act of storytelling, Cleghorn combines the need for affordable housing as being met by churches with more property than they need and the resurrection that is the result. With wisdom, vision, and a compassionate commitment to helping others, Cleghorn shares his personal story as it intersects with the call of Christ to home the houseless and care for those who are without the basic necessities of life. All in the name of the Christ who calls us to care and to act."

—Jimmie R. Hawkins, Director of Advocacy for the Presbyterian Church (U.S.A.)

Building Belonging

Building Belonging is designed for congregational, communal, or small-group use. To assist these groups as they develop their own plans for creating community and housing neighbors, we've designed a free, downloadable congregational guide that provides a road map to enact the innovative strategies outlined in the book. Visit **www.wjkbooks.com/BuildingBelonging** to download this resource.

Building Belonging

*The Church's Call to Create Community
and House Our Neighbors*

JOHN CLEGHORN

WESTMINSTER
JOHN KNOX PRESS
LOUISVILLE • KENTUCKY

First edition
Published by Westminster John Knox Press
Louisville, Kentucky

24 25 26 27 28 29 30 31 32 33—10 9 8 7 6 5 4 3 2 1

Book design by Sharon Adams
Cover design by Kevin van der Leek

Library of Congress Cataloging-in-Publication Data

Names: Cleghorn, John, Rev. Dr., author.
Title: Building belonging : the church's call to create community and house our neighbors / John Cleghorn.
Description: First edition. | Louisville, Kentucky : Westminster John Knox Press, [2024] | Summary: "Readers will be inspired to look at the unfolding narrative of unaffordable housing in a new way and be inspired to shape their ministry to harness all available resources to foster access and justice by housing neighbors"-- Provided by publisher.
Identifiers: LCCN 2024035223 (print) | LCCN 2024035224 (ebook) | ISBN 9780664268503 (paperback) | ISBN 9781646984039 (ebook)
Subjects: LCSH: Church work with the homeless--North Carolina--Charlotte. | Church work with the poor--North Carolina--Charlotte. | Housing--Religious aspects--Christianity.
Classification: LCC BV4456 .C54 2024 (print) | LCC BV4456 (ebook) | DDC 261.8/3250975676--dc23/eng/20240905
LC record available at https://lccn.loc.gov/2024035223
LC ebook record available at https://lccn.loc.gov/2024035224

Most Westminster John Knox Press books are available at special quantity discounts when purchased in bulk by corporations, organizations, and special-interest groups. For more information, please e-mail SpecialSales@wjkbooks.com.

Proceeds from the sale of this book will be donated to Easter's Home at Caldwell Presbyterian Church.

Contents

Acknowledgments

The spaces of my home church are always only a comforting memory away: the preschool room where my classmates and I played, learned our letters, and took naps on thinly padded, foldout plastic mats; the choir rehearsal room where our devoted director kept us boys in line with a stern look and, when necessary, a sharp word; the lawn where, after choir practice, we would gather and wait for the senior minister, Rev. Dr. Allison Williams, to fling open his second-floor window and toss candy down to us as we waited for our rides home.

There was the musty Boy Scout hut, the long, linoleum-tiled hallway perfect for playing floor hockey with my best friend, Bill Love, until someone on the church staff ran us off. There was the fellowship hall where, as little boys, Bill and I darted and weaved between the adults as they mingled during coffee hour after worship. (It's a wonder we never got scalded.) A few years later in that same room as a youth elder, I turned eighteen years old during a marathon session meeting that ran past midnight.

I remember the secret stairway behind the chancel and the phone booth–size A/V room tucked into the walls behind the organist, where I took my turn at the sound equipment for worship. (As far as I know, I somehow avoided switching off the preacher's microphone mid-sermon.) I can still see the pews from behind the lectern in the chancel where I offered a stumbling senior sermon and, decades later, where I stood to eulogize my mother. In those spaces, the love and nurture of the body of Christ enfolded me. I was held, formed, and taught by mentors, who made the church a place of community and safekeeping amid life's storms and celebrations.

As a boy, I knew vaguely of a stately home on an adjoining property the church owned. There, out of sight and the awareness of most, the church partnered with an agency to provide shelter for unwed mothers. In that quiet way, Trinity Presbyterian Church in Atlanta foreshadowed what this book is about: an emerging movement of faith communities that are providing shelter, building housing, and offering resurrection of a sort, all of it as "room in the inn" for those unwelcomed in other spaces.

My childhood years at Trinity came amid the good times for most churches. Parking lots and pews were filled on Sundays. Ample church buildings erected for the church's heyday hummed through the week with gatherings and activities. Congregants gave generously, and church life was abundant in almost all ways.

Those days are now past. Many if not most church parking lots have far more spaces than cars, and the pews are generally more empty than full. Church budgets are tighter than ever, and maintaining aging church buildings demands as much or more money than any other expense. Forty million Americans have left church in the last quarter century, a trend that isn't slowing. In the next decade or two, tens of thousands of churches will close. Churches almost everywhere seek the secrets of transformation of their mission and ministries. Leaders are asking hard questions and confronting financial realities. Still, in it all there is resurrection, new life, new possibilities, new hope.

As I offer a few words of appreciation and acknowledgment for what led to this book, it seems appropriate to start with my childhood church. It shaped me, offered belonging, and planted the seeds of my calling to ministry. In saying "Thank you," I bracket my childhood church with the church I now serve, Caldwell Presbyterian, which has also shaped me. It is always teaching, stretching, and reforming me, including through our shared ten-year odyssey to provide on-campus apartments for those who have been chronically homeless. Caldwell's journey inspired this book, and the congregation encouraged it.

That dream wouldn't have happened without those in the Caldwell congregation who laid the financial cornerstone years ago. Several friends, mine and the church's, also contributed substantially early on to the capital campaign that set the foundation and encouraged our cross-shaped folly. So many Caldwell members have labored to make it happen, including Gina Shell, the late Johnny Johnson and Richard Harrison, Eddy Capote, Rob Hammock, Elli Dai, Lisa Thompson, Jeff Brown, Lori Thomas, Rick Rogers, and others. I apologize for inevitably leaving others out.

The team at Roof Above, Charlotte's leading agency addressing homelessness and housing, also believed in our dream. My friends and co-laborers at DreamKey Partners, chiefly the unwavering Fred Dodson, have faithfully kindled the notion of Caldwell's housing ministry for more than a decade. I wish to thank the Louisville Institute for its guidance and financial grant that funded my travel for researching this book during the summer of 2022. I am deeply grateful for the many pastors and church leaders who received me that summer and sat for the interviews that fill these pages.

I also owe my adopted hometown of Charlotte and its citizens, from the visionary and powerful to those on its margins who struggle in the shadows of the city's affluence. The city has been a learning lab for me for four decades through my various professions. This book is, in part, a letter of loving protest over what our city has gotten wrong and, yet, a witness of living hope in the best part of the city's nature and aspiration.

Without the interest of Westminster John Knox Press and the insightful mind and needed touch of my editor, Bridgett Green, the book would have fallen far short. Thanks to them for believing in the project. Charlotte's public theologian, Rev. Greg Jarrell, has been a guide and walking partner. Most of all, without the abiding patience of my family and the support of so many friends, the book would not have happened.

As important as any, this book is written in tribute to a woman named Easter and the others who were enslaved by the Caldwell family on an antebellum plantation north of Charlotte. Their abduction; their unpaid, forced labor; and their blood, sweat, tears, and unimaginably harsh days made the fortune that was ultimately left to our church (which was then named for the Caldwell family). By naming its housing and supportive services community "Easter's Home," Caldwell Presbyterian Church prays that our unhoused neighbors who come to live on our campus will know a kind of liberation, dignity, citizenhood, and new beginning that Easter was never offered. In the same breath, we pray that this ministry will liberate and equip us to dismantle the sins of structural poverty, racism, and exclusion.

For all, thanks be to God.

Chapter One

Making God's House a Home

On a humid, Friday summer evening in the nation's capital, Westminster Presbyterian Church is filling up. With all the city's options for entertainment, about 200 people stream into a funky, 170-year-old church in a working-class neighborhood. It's jazz night again, and a popular group with a hot saxophonist draws folks from across the city looking to reconnect with the music and friends and let off a little steam. Jazz helps do that.

The musicians plunge in and cruise through the first set. On the final note, the host steps to the microphone and invites applause, and the appreciative crowd generously responds. He feels the mood and reads the room. "There's something spiritual about the way these guys play," he says. "You are a blessing to them, and they are here to bless you." A banner on the lawn declares, "Jesus and Justice: Building Rhythm Together for Christ's Love," and Westminster Presbyterian uses the language of the arts to reach its mixed-income, racially complex, tree-covered neighborhood.

But all of that is changing—dramatically. As with jazz, creating a thriving church is now all about reading the moment, adapting, and improvising. So Rev. Brian Hamilton and his diverse congregation of 120 are working on their biggest riff yet. In a $180-million act of faith, the church is tearing itself down so that it can build itself back in a form that its neighborhood needs.

The congregation will move out and level the entire church campus, emptying most of a city block. It will rebuild and return, renewed and re-equipped to serve its neighbors with mixed-income housing and community and creative spaces. Plans call for a smaller sanctuary better fitted for the current congregation, gathering and fellowship space, a recording studio for emerging musicians, a studio for exhibiting local artists' work. Rising above will be a tower of affordable apartments—102 units for families and 123 for seniors. Long-term plans call for a second tower. In a city where housing costs are soaring, the housing Westminster builds will help current residents stay in the neighborhood.

The fruit of years of dreaming and planning, the new campus will enable Westminster to spread the gospel's lessons of love and justice to its community in ways that build on the identity the congregation has labored to establish. Along the winding journey, Hamilton has watched the congregation learn powerful lessons. It's drawing new energy that springs from bold, audacious undertakings. It's practicing a faith tradition of sacrificing its past to unleash a new future in solidarity with its neighbors.

The transformation comes with countless complexities, steep challenges, and frequent headaches. Hamilton knows the cultural headwinds that churches everywhere face—as well as the tendency by most congregations to avoid risk and cling to old ways, even unto death. Still, he smiles at the thought of Westminster's future.

As crazy as Westminster's particular vision may seem, he speaks for churches everywhere amid the fast-shifting realities of organized religion in the early twenty-first century. "Churches have to reinvent themselves, and that is what this is," he says. "This is an opportunity to create a whole new identity, a new reality. The congregation has come to realize it has the capacity to do this."

About 350 miles to the south, Newell Presbyterian sits comfortably on slightly rolling land on the edge of Charlotte, North Carolina. Not that long ago the surrounding fields were covered with corn and contented dairy cattle. Now the land is laced with rows of tract homes that have popped up outside a fast-growing city. Newell's congregation numbers about 90 people from a range of ages and backgrounds. As with many churches, its annual budget is tight. In recent years, elders started including a line item labeled "leap of faith" for the amount of money it hopes will come in so that income and expenses come near balancing out. Newell's pastor, North Carolina–born Rev. Matt Conner, uses a Texas phrase in describing the church's reality. "We're an 'all hat and no cattle' congregation," he says.

What Conner's congregation may lack in money, it doesn't lack in faith. At a gut-check session meeting (the kind more and more churches are having), the elders confronted the truth that about a third of the church budget went to pay for the maintenance of its aging buildings. Then the congregation took a long, prayerful walk around its ample campus. On Ascension Sunday, when congregations consider the question the angels asked Jesus' disciples—"Why are you standing around looking up at the sky?"—Newell looked at its abundance of property. "We asked, 'What if our biggest liability is really our biggest asset?'" Conner recalls.

That question led to the congregation's plan to use five of its ten acres to create a village of about fifty affordable, for-sale homes. The plan calls for a mix of townhomes and duet cottages for those earning 60 to 80 percent of the area's median income, a widely used measurement of financial capacity.[1] In Newell's area in 2023, that was between $41,880 and $55,850 for one person and $59,820 and $79,750 for a family of four.[2]

After listening deeply to the needs of its city and community, the congregation felt called to partner with a nonprofit agency that serves individuals and families impacted by incarceration and/or deportation. Housing, health care, employment opportunity, transportation—the list of their needs is long and daunting. Clear-eyed about their limitations, Newell decided to go all in on housing. "There are so many ways churches can reimagine their underutilized property for the sake of the gospel and for their communities," Conner says. "This was the particular path we feel God laid out before us."

Income from the land-sale portion of the project will annually supplement the congregation's tithes and offerings. Conner believes that more important than the restoration of its financial stability, however, its missional identity will be renewed as it recreates the "house of God" to be a new community. "We saw our land as a 'field of dreams' to help people put down roots, build a sense of community, and have a place of their own," he says.

Why This Book?

When I entered ministry in 2007, I would have never imagined the need for a book that connects the nation's deep housing crisis, the ongoing erosion of community across America, and the need for almost every church to rethink its existence and ministry. But who could have anticipated the social forces that have influenced the nation and reshaped the outlook for organized religion? Yet however unimaginable these developments were, the church is called to consider its highest form of service "for such a time as this" in every time.

Even if your church has never considered its relationship to housing, this book tells the stories of people and congregations that demonstrate what is needed in congregations everywhere today: clear-eyed assessment of the state of the neighborhood church, deep listening and unblinking analysis of what's needed in our communities, and the courage to discern and pursue outrageous dreams (of all kinds) for ministry that manifests the love and justice of Jesus Christ in meeting the most basic of human needs.

This book, then, is for those who are considering a career in ministry but know the landscape is shifting dramatically for congregations almost everywhere in America. It is for students and dreamers. It is for established pastors looking for ideas that can energize a stuck congregation. It offers case studies of the possible. It is for leaders in all the places where hard questions must be asked. It is for risk-taking, gospel-driven entrepreneurs who trust God with God's property. It is for those who haven't given up on the idea of community.

It is also for the congregations that have taken up the journey of exploring their call to house their neighbors. It is for city planners and elected leaders looking for new solutions in unexpected places. It is for Thomas, an aging amputee in a wheelchair who sleeps outside near our church, and the millions of others who need America to do better by them.

It is written with the preposterous notion that despite the scale of our national homelessness crisis—18 out of every 10,000 Americans is unhoused—this is actually a crisis that we *can* fix.[3] Along the way, the church can reassert its moral and practical leadership in the sight of all those who have grown disillusioned with the church as a place of far more talk than action.

Crisis is, admittedly, a shopworn word. Still, the church might consider the definition from the Cambridge Dictionary that a crisis is "an extremely difficult or dangerous point in a situation."[4]

What exactly is this "difficult situation"? What changes can lead to recovery?

Three Crises . . . and a Call

A "polycrisis" is the simultaneous occurrence of multiple catastrophic events. That description might sound a bit extreme, but let's consider the facts. In almost every urb, suburb, exurb, and rural crossroads in America, the church sits at the convergence of three crises. Perhaps at that exact spot, however, there is a new call and new life that powerfully proclaims the gospel's resurrection story.

Crisis #1: Housing Affordability

A spiraling affordable-housing crisis now touches every state and county and all types of communities, creating record levels of housing insecurity in one of the world's richest nations. The crisis is in plain sight well beyond big cities. Americans name the housing crisis as one of their most urgent concerns.

According to the standard measures of affordability, there is no U.S. county where a full-time, minimum-wage worker can afford to rent or own a one-bedroom dwelling. Stop and reread that last sentence. That is an indictment of both wages and housing. Nationwide, nearly half of all renting households spend an unsustainable amount of their income on rent, a figure that is only expected to rise. This is not only a big-city issue. Four out of ten rural renters are cost-burdened (meaning they spend 30 percent or more of their income on housing), and 21 percent are severely cost-burdened (spending 50 percent or more of their income on housing). And the housing cost burden for rural households is deepening.[5] The prosperity of mid-tier cities, such as Austin, Texas; Tacoma, Washington; Nashville, Tennessee; Durham, North Carolina; Columbus, Ohio; and Charlotte, North Carolina, is pushing out those with middle and low incomes. These are neighbors who work in the service and hospitality industries, who fix cars and practice the trades that keep our homes repaired and our lawns neat and trimmed.

Compounding the housing squeeze is the reality that many earn at or near the minimum wage, which remains stubbornly low relative to across-the-board price increases for the basics of living. At $7.25 an hour, the rate set in 2009, the federal minimum wage is half or less what many consider a *living* wage. Nearly half of all workers earn an hourly wage that lags what is needed to rent a one-bedroom apartment in decent condition at fair-market rates.[6]

The impact of our housing crisis falls heaviest on the most vulnerable, and you'll find them where you may not expect. In the last two decades, poverty in America reached a tipping point, concentrating more poor residents in suburbs than cities. America's long-standing wealth divide is widening, and the middle class is continuing to shrink. As with almost all things in America, people of color face deep-seated disparities, causing them too often to work twice as hard for half as much just to stay sheltered.

Underneath it all is a vast shortage of housing of every type, at any price. It will take decades to reverse, if it can be reversed. For those of modest and lower incomes, as has been said, finding housing in America is like playing musical chairs. When the music stops, those who may lack the agency, agility, time, and social and financial capacity to find affordable housing lose out.

Crisis #2: Implosion of Community

A second crisis is the deepening implosion of community across America. From small towns to big cities, from civic organizations to neighborhood associations, from parent-teacher organizations to Sunday school classes, our muscles for creating and sustaining community have shriveled. In 1967, Rev. Dr. Martin Luther King Jr.

asked whether America was moving toward chaos or community. Chaos has had a good run. Community lost out.

Three decades later, researcher and political scientist Robert Putnam documented the decline in social capital, the rise of toxic individualism, and the danger of our "bowling alone" in the hyper-fragmentation across lines of ideology, race, class, perspective, and experience. In the social media–inflamed years that followed, our polarization compounded at every level, from neighborhood to the nation's capital.

As America moves steadily toward its majority-minority future, when there will be no racial majority, white supremacy and Christian nationalism have marched out of the shadows and into the mainstream. Some seek shelter by burrowing even more deeply within their tribes, finding affirmation among those who think just like they do. People with financial resources have segregated themselves into exclusive gated and walled communities. Some have moved out of the country altogether or at least purchased some form of an "escape" property somewhere in case of civil breakdown. Gun sales have soared, hinting at armed conflict of some sort.

Somewhere amid the decline of the middle class, vast class disparities, lagging public policy, profit-hungry real-estate development and resegregated cities and towns, we forgot what community can look like and why we need it.

This doesn't seem like what God has in mind. In his letter to the church at Ephesus, Paul declares that we are saved through faith precisely to be about the good work that God has planned for us (Eph. 2:8–10). We are, Paul instructs, to pursue this way of life, to do these good works *together*, in community. We yearn to belong and are created to be in community that transcends our most base, tribal, survival instincts. Paul writes:

> You're no longer wandering exiles. This kingdom of faith is now your home country. You're no longer strangers or outsiders. You *belong* here, with as much right to the name Christian as anyone. God is building a home. He's using us all—irrespective of how we got here—in what he is building. He used the apostles and prophets for the foundation. Now he's using you, fitting you in

brick by brick, stone by stone, with Christ Jesus as the cornerstone that holds all the parts together. We see it taking shape day after day—a holy temple built by God, all of us built into it, a temple in which God is quite at home. (Eph. 2:19–22, *The Message*)

Therefore, in our churches, neighborhoods, and houses of faith, we are called to be the kind of masons who are equipped to rebuild community brick by brick and stone by stone, all upheld by the one cornerstone, Christ. When community is set squarely on the love and justice Christ taught, died, and rose for, it can bear the weight of all our similarities and differences, agreements and disagreements. When stacked and fitted together and resting on common ground, we can rebuild true community.

Crisis #3: Christianity's Great Reordering

The third crisis is that of organized religion in America. In short, from its mid-twentieth-century apex, organized religion, principally Christianity, has moved from the center of American life to the margins. Too often sweeping change inspires only fear. Too often we see a *crisis*, what the dictionary terms "a time of great disagreement, confusion, or suffering,"[7] only as a reason to freeze, isolate, and hunker down.

In terms of numbers, to the degree they matter, the church's decline is nothing new. It is generations old. Some people describe themselves as spiritual but not religious. Many grew disillusioned by the homophobia, hypocrisy, and intolerance displayed in too many houses of worship. The rise of evangelicalism and its barefaced identification with extreme politics, politicians, and ideologies have made the term *Christian* a pejorative in many settings.

The COVID-19 pandemic intensified and accelerated the challenges facing organized religion. Congregations already slow to respond to the changing religious landscape before COVID emerged from it facing even more daunting uncertainty about what church life, worship, and participation would be. Little was left of the tightly knit church communities of the twentieth century. Existential questions face thousands of congregations. A record number—as many as one in three by one estimate—won't survive the coming years.[8]

These and other forces pile weighty pressures on church pastors and leaders already exhausted, if not burned out entirely, from trying to reinvent church and keep their congregations off life support. Understandably, deacons, elders, and church volunteers of all kinds risk seeing only scarcity rather than opportunities for fresh ways to serve their communities.

What Call, Then?

My former colleague in ministry at Caldwell, Rev. Gail Henderson-Belsito, always knew how to remind us that, however challenging the outlook, God is never through. "But God ," she loves to preach. God is present at the convergence of these three crises. There the Lord is at work in this movement of churches that are building housing and, thereby, returning their properties to biblical meanings of sanctuary and shelter.

By looking anew at their material and spiritual assets, congregations are responding to the affordable housing crisis in their locales by making God's land a literal home to help some of the millions of those at risk in the nation's housing crisis. Along the way, they are learning new expressions of their faith and meanings of community. They are unlocking new resources and realizing the vitality that has long evaded tiring church leaders. They are liberated to extend the gospel in new and enlivening ways.

As they see through the fresh lenses that accompany the radical transformation of dying to self, more and more churches are reimagining their identity, mission, property, and future. Practically every week as I researched and wrote this book, I learned of another church that is building housing. These possibilities stem from what God has asked and expected of God's people (i.e., everyone) all along, especially those who have controlled land and property. So these crises of housing and community land literally at the front door of churches large and small, urban, suburban, and rural. In our Holy Scripture, property and land echo as part of God's call to build just, inclusive, mutual, interdependent, and holistic communities.

Consider this: The church at large in the United States controls hundreds of thousands of acres of land and hundreds of millions of dollars in property. One study by the University of California at Berkeley Terner Center for Housing Innovation found that in California alone there are 38,000 acres of religious land across 10,000 parcels that are potentially developable. No such comprehensive estimate for the nation as a whole yet exists. But you can extrapolate the potential in California to the country and let your imagination run. A 2019 estimate by one denomination, the United Church of Christ, is that between 75 and 100 churches close per week. Extrapolating from that number and using other data, another church official estimates that 100,000 church properties will have been sold by 2030.[9]

With a focus on housing neighbors and building community, the church is uniquely positioned to respond. The call to heal the nation with more housing and enriched communities comes from within and beyond the church. "On its own, the private market cannot and will not build and operate homes affordable to extremely low-income families," the National Low Income Housing Coalition reported in 2022. "Only a sustained public commitment can ensure that the lowest income renters, who are disproportionately people of color, have stable, accessible, and affordable homes."[10]

Is Koinonia Still Possible?

The church strives to build the beloved community, to bear witness to God's entrance into our broken and hurting world in the person of Christ Jesus, the prophet without a home who identified himself with the poor, the unhoused, the oppressed, and the rejected. Koinonia— a community in God that gathers those of many different stories, perspectives, experiences, ideas, and opinions—is still possible! It isn't easy, but the church has never been called to do only easy things. Can we wade into this surely messy but life-giving space? Can we see anew the God who created us in such splendid diversity, meant not to live apart but to grow together? Can we still be the beloved community that God in Christ came to usher in and commanded us to spread?

Perhaps it is exactly the scandal of Easter that answers those questions. Perhaps it is our claim that God came and dwelt with us, as one of us, before taking the sins of the world to the cross and liberating us all to respond with all we are and all we have. God's intimate entry into the human condition shows God's desire to be proximate to us in every way. Christ's promise to be with us "to the end of the age" (Matt. 28:20) is our ready source of courage and commitment.

Will we respond to God's grace-infused mandate? Can we respond by growing more proximate to others who may not be in our neighborhood, tribe, club, race, or class? Can we find ways to bridge the canyons that divide our neighborhoods, towns, cities, and nation? Can we rediscover the life-giving blessings of belonging and community?

The gospel insists on a bias for possibility over problems, hope over fear, abundance over scarcity, resurrection life over death, and community over chaos. Maybe, even while it faces its own present challenges, the church can still raise its voice with visible action instead of just more words.

The church's most overlooked possibility, its open secret you might say, is that it owns or otherwise controls a treasure of property and real estate in prime locations in almost every town and city. In cities, suburbs, and small towns, congregations reside on valuable and well-located blocks and corners. Church property is the most valuable land in many communities. All of it is entrusted to congregations only through the grace and abundance of the God who instructs us to build community.

The plain truth is that many, perhaps most, of our churches will likely never be as full as they once were. Equally true, even for thriving churches, is that most church campuses were built for a very different time in Christendom. Some congregations are already counting the days, months, or years before their doors may close forever. Thriving and well-financed churches know, too, that their property is as much burden as it is blessing. In the years to come, church governing bodies will be immersed in the real estate business, presenting pivotal decisions relating to millions of dollars worth of property. That presents a raft of new responsibilities for "church people" already faced with locating resurrection in a world of "nones" and "dones" with religion, much less tackling problems like a housing crisis or mastering yearslong, complex real estate development possibilities. Whatever is to come of the local church, it stands at the convergence of its own existential crisis, a national cry for community, and a housing crisis that, directly or indirectly, shapes every American neighborhood.

My Vantage Point

Through three different professions and decades of community engagement, I've had a close vantage point on Charlotte's housing and real estate story for the last forty years. In the 1980s, as a business writer for the city's newspaper, the *Charlotte Observer*, I covered housing and residential real estate development for a living. In those same years, wearing the hat of a Presbyterian elder, I sat in the cool basement of Uptown Charlotte's historic St. Peter's Catholic Church, where an ecumenical and interfaith group grappled with the earliest phases of the city's emerging challenge of homelessness.

In the 1990s and early 2000s, I worked on the city's streets and in its neighborhoods. In one case, I served on a racially integrated, multichurch team invited by the residents of the Seversville neighborhood to explore ways to stabilize that community, then a low-income, Black community of rental and owner-occupied homes battling crime and neglect, including by the city of Charlotte's public works department. We worked alongside its residents and through local schools, churches, and other community anchors. When the partnership concluded its work, homeowners in Seversville felt safer, more stable, and ready to sustain the momentum it had built. Neighborhood leaders expressed their gratitude. But what did we set in motion? In the ensuing years, Seversville has been subsumed by waves of gentrification and displacement sweeping over the city. I am left to consider "the law of unintended consequences" and the mighty power of the real estate industry.

Most recently, I've occupied a different perch—seventeen years of ministry leading a diverse, dynamic, missional, justice-seeking congregation. I've watched, learned, and continued to advocate for fairness and compassion in a city that's often busier growing than caring. I've witnessed the unfolding of my church's dream to build affordable housing for the chronically homeless on our campus in an affluent neighborhood.

I came to Charlotte in 1984 right out of college for many of the same qualities it still bears: a can-do attitude, a sense of opportunity, potential, energy, and hope. It is a city of churches and other houses of faith where the faith community has for decades been active in addressing social issues. Compared to some of its Southern peers, it looks forward far more than backward. Looking ahead is good, as long as it takes in the lessons of the past.

I've sunk my heart into my adopted hometown. I've worked closely with some of the city's most powerful corporate leaders and elite families. I've also been given the gift of transformative relationships with some of the city's most impoverished, vulnerable, and oppressed families.

Through my time in Charlotte, scales have fallen from my eyes—the eyes of a white, affluent, cisgender, straight, educated male. I see more clearly how the city inflicted injustices in its march toward progress. It left far too many out of decision-making and has, to date, failed to repair harm done to generations of its most vulnerable residents. Today some of the city's aging lions of civic leadership confess their blindness and oversight. The damage remains. As it becomes the next Atlanta, today's Charlotte still struggles in its search for identity and shared vision.

My journey informs and compels the research and ideas behind this book. The pages that follow are framed by the three interlocking crises facing the local church and how God may be speaking through them. Chapter 2 looks to Scripture and finds God's ideas about economy, property, place, and belonging. Chapter 3 takes a closer look at the "polycrisis" in which today's churches exist. Chapter 4 invites readers to examine their own city or community through a case study of one city—mine. We look at the social, cultural, and racial factors that helped create Charlotte's housing crisis. We also look at how Charlotte churches have responded to the crisis with multiple housing initiatives that make the city a showcase for the movement. Chapter 5 broadens the lens to trace the history of the church housing movement across the country, profiling what congregations are doing to make "many dwelling places" in direct response to the needs of their neighborhoods. Chapter 6 concludes the book with a review of the movement—how churches can consider their own possibilities and what hurdles and other factors will dictate the movement's success.

Along the way, I will share my congregation's ten-year journey to build affordable housing. The story of Caldwell Presbyterian's vision, perseverance, and spunk reflects that of many other congregations that make up this movement, drawing from deep faith and courage and belief in resurrection—theirs and their new neighbors'—and in the meaning of community.

All these stories invite church members and their neighbors to think in new ways about legacy and liberation from costly, aging properties and traditional, outdated mission and ministry. Along the way, the congregations forming this movement tell inspiring stories of transformation and a shift from a mindset of scarcity to one of abundance.

From Los Angeles to New York, Seattle to Atlanta, churches are transforming excess parking spaces into villages of tiny homes as transitional housing for those coming off the streets. In communities where even middle-class people can't afford to live, some are building townhomes for working families. Some are providing permanent supportive housing for those with disabilities, addictions, and mental health challenges. Some build mixed-income housing to create multigenerational communities that blend seniors with young families. Some build affordable apartment towers where residents can move in and stay for as long as needed.

From the perspective of struggling or stagnated congregations, sales or leases of their land provide financial capital that buys their congregations reprieve from immediate pressures and time to dream big. Pastors and church leaders suddenly realize how the luxury of imagination and liberation leads to new visions of ministry.

Beyond the church, similar-minded partners are adapting to advance the movement. Elected officials and city administrators under pressures of their own to alleviate the housing crisis are awakening to partner with congregations to put housing on church campuses. Private and nonprofit real estate developers are learning to "speak church." Banks have launched pilot programs to work with congregations to finance housing on church campuses. What began as a spark is a growing, gospel-shaped revival of church and community. "There is now an intentionality to work with the faith community," says David Bowers, an ordained minister and vice president for Faith-Based Development Initiative for Enterprise Community Partners. "We're at a tipping point. There is so much potential."

God's people, however, look first not to the realms of finance or law or public policy. God calls us to remember our baptismal vows—that we are to die to our old selves. To frame it more theologically, in the words of scholar/preacher Fred Craddock, "The question is not whether the church is dying, but whether it is giving its life for the world."[11]

Chapter Two

God's Ideas about Land, Shelter, and Economy

"It's the economy, stupid."

With that memorable phrase, the sharp-tongued Cajun politico James Carville advised Bill Clinton's presidential run in 1992. Carville knew Clinton's penchant for big ideas and his tendency to address too many issues at once. Today's church needs its own memorable reminder: God's economy is not America's economy. The church forgets how *God's* economy differs from the economy we encounter in the world, especially in America. Scripture tells us God has ideas about land, property, and shelter that are different from what contemporary real estate markets demonstrate. Perhaps refocusing on God's divine design might frame how churches and their leaders view their property and its possibilities.

A God-infused, God-shaped economy barely resembles what most think of as the American Dream or a pure market economy. The word *economy* comes from a combination of the ancient Greek words *oikos* (meaning "household") and *nomos* (meaning "law" or "management"). Thus, in God's story, the idea of *oikonomia* outlines how we are to manage our family household—its resources and how they are shared and distributed. The household, in God's design, is to be managed to give and sustain life for all who live in community under God.

From stories as early as those about Abram and Sarai, we learn that God's economy is about using what we have out of a sense of hospitality and abundance—even if some, especially the host, have to get by with a little less.

In Scripture, land represents a promised place freely given, not taken as a legal or economic right and used for exclusion. Exodus tells of the Israelites' enslavement under Pharaoh, without a place of their own, reduced to hard labor benefiting only the few. Then we learn of their liberation, God's promise of provision in the wilderness, and their delivery to the promised land—a vivid picture of God's intentions even now.

The remainder of the Pentateuch, the Old Testament's first five books assigned by tradition to Moses the emancipator, enshrined God's additional commands. God's people were to balance individual need with the common good, with the common good always as the priority so that all would have at least enough. The prophets warned God's people when they trampled the vulnerable and indulged in material excess, including their ways and means of worship. Wisdom poetry called them back to praising the Lord in all things, including using and sharing all that comes as a gift from God.

The sweep of the Old Testament follows God's people in their search for a home. It documents all the ways God's people get it wrong in distributing and governing the land God gives. Over and over they turn away from God's design to follow worldly models of leadership and the distribution of goods and property. (Yet, just as often, God responds to the mistaken Israelites with grace.)

Particular Guidance: God's Instructions at the Border

In considering God's design for the use of land, property, and place, Old Testament scholar Walter Brueggemann draws deeply from one specific moment for the children of Israel. As told in Deuteronomy, the Israelites have almost completed their exodus out of slavery and through the wilderness under God's care. They are gathered at the Jordan River, about to enter the promised land. They will leave one side of the Jordan as the formerly enslaved, fleeing their oppressors with little. By the time they reach the opposite riverbank, they will be gifted with the land God gives them—a place of vast abundance, all a nation would ever need. There they pause to listen to God.

"The Jordan crossing represents the moment of the most radical transformation of any historical person or group, to the moment of empowerment or enlandment, the decisive event of being turfed and at home for the first time," Brueggemann writes.[1]

The land is a pure gift, radical grace. But it comes with divine strings attached—a covenant with God that will bind Israel to enjoy and use the land on God's terms. Those terms are laid out in the law God gives Israel, and they are clear. The land and its fruits are to be shared with all and for all. Specifically, Israel is to use its bounty for the care of the poor, the ones among its number who are unlanded, just as all of Israel had been. These are variously characterized: the poor (Exod. 23:6; Deut. 15:7–11), the stranger (Deut. 10:19), the widow and orphan (Deut. 24:19–22), and the Levite (Deut. 14:27). The people on this diverse list have one common feature: They have no standing ground in the community. They are without land and so without power and so without dignity. They have "no allotment or inheritance" (Deut. 14:27). The landed at the boundary are tasked with the care of those when they come to the land. It is one of the duties that go with covenanted land. It keeps the land as covenanted reality; those who seem to have no claim must be honored and cared for.[2]

This is not all that comes with the land. In addition to responsibility comes temptation to forget God's arrangement and how Israel came into the land in the first place. Land brings power and is a source of seduction. It brings the risk of idolatry, the idolatry of assuming that the land's abundance is only for some and not for others and that land is to be "managed" by humanity rather than received and enjoyed as a gift of God. The covenant of land requires, Brueggemann says, a "peculiar conscious." Land is an "opportunity to pervert justice" and a temptation to private well-being "[that] is a way of death," Brueggemann adds. "Then take heed, lest you forget Yahweh, who brought you out of the land of Egypt, out of the house of bondage" (Deut. 6:12).[3]

The Lord's truth then still applies. We will return to the Lord's instructions for Israel at the border in Deuteronomy 6 to consider them for our day and to see how far America has wandered off course. We will consider whether, even in small ways, our well-landed churches might undergo the same kind of radical transformation God required of Israel on the banks of the Jordan.

New Testament Paradigms
for Land, Property, and Space

God's instructions about the use of land, property, and resources continue in a new light in the New Testament. In Christ, God reasserted the announcement of abundance over scarcity in radical ways. Embodying God's upside-down reign, Christ redefined hierarchy and demonstrated a more just use of resources for the poor, the suffering, the outcast, the prisoner, the widow, and the child.

Repeatedly, Christ warned religious leaders and everyday people about material accumulation, both individually and institutionally. When the Temple was used purely as a place of business, Jesus turned it upside down to make it right side up again (John 2:15). Jesus befriended, walked with, and dined with the wealthy and the tax collectors, who were often rich in material wealth but poor in spirit. He never failed to remind them of how God's economics are to work. In Acts 2, we see God's economy at a glance, as the first Christ followers swore to share all things and live from a common purse. We watch as the new Jesus movement spread the word of a new way of being community—living out of a common purse and even selling property and possessions to give to those in need (Acts 2:44–45).

At the center of these biblical truths are prickly questions for congregations and denominations with valuable property who are facing new questions about mission, stewardship, and legacy. Where does an individual's or a congregation's freedom over property end and God's original design begin? How is property used to give life and not deprive it from others?

Who decides questions of church property ownership and purpose when we read words like those in Isaiah 65:21 that express God's hope for the day when all are housed, when the people "shall live in the houses they build, and eat fruit of the vineyards they plant"? Is property meant for all, for inclusion, or are land and property simply a form of the spoils of war and competition to be used as a means of exclusion?

God's economy invites us to be both practical and theological. In *God the Economist: The Doctrine of God and Political Economy*, theologian M. Douglas Meeks frames the doctrine of the Trinity in ways congregations as property owners/controllers might consider:

> God is not a self-possessor. God is rather a community, a community of persons united in giving themselves to each other and to the world. God is not a closed self, acting autonomously without regard to impact on the community as when God is worshiped as an absolute private property owner. The Triune God is the inexhaustible life that the three persons share in common, in which they are present with one another, for one another, and in one another.[4]

In all matters of life and death, Christ gives us God's economic design. We celebrate the sacrament of Communion by taking, blessing, breaking, and sharing bread in Christ's memory, as Christ's provision. In baptism, we die to our old selves that we may live as God intends—in community that is to look like family, not private islands of existence or tribal enclaves of like-minded hoarders. In everything, God's people look to the meaning of Easter and resurrection. Christ's life-giving death and Easter triumph call us to empty ourselves for the sake of others. In so doing, we receive new life. In the doing, we are made new, liberated from the weight of living only for ourselves or only for our congregations. We can rediscover the richest meaning of community.

Despite all this grounding, the ascendance of modern thought in Western societies in the seventeenth and eighteenth centuries led to the divorce of God's rules from those of markets and economies. The church forgot God's *oikonomia*, how the church is to model the management of God's household. In many places, the church conveniently aligned itself with the ways of affluence, competition, a scarcity mindset, and support for individual freedoms over property. The church became a means of convenient charity more than inconvenient justice. The expansive campuses built in the mid-twentieth century that included acres of land, large sanctuaries, and education wings that now are far more empty than full are the legacy and, increasingly, the burden of congregations coast to coast.

Inevitably, churches carry out their lives and mission in the context of capitalism. Capitalists built expansive church campuses. Capitalism can also produce wealth that some give away. To be sure, when practiced with restraint and a basic moral compass, capitalism can create resources to share. But capitalism can also act like a runaway train with no brakeman. Recent decades have exposed the toxic inclinations and excesses of unchecked, late-stage capitalism. The wealth divide between haves and have-nots has deepened into historic dimensions, creating what many have begun to think is a permanent underclass. The racial wealth gap remains, counting about one dollar in the household wealth of Black households for every ten dollars for white households.

Jesus doesn't oppose money categorically—only the idolatrous love of it. The apostle Paul wrote that God commands those who are rich in the present age to also be rich in good works. They are to be generous and ready to share to live a "life that really is life" (1 Tim. 6:19). Money, property, land, and power can be used to build up the beloved community or to tear it down. Shane Claiborne writes, "The idolatry of wealth doesn't only compromise our relationship with God; it destroys community and makes abundant life impossible. But if we disarm the power of money and set it free to build the beloved community, then it can be used for redemption, for restoration, for the liberation of the oppressed, and for building relationships."[5]

Unfortunately, a spirit of generosity doesn't describe how many people think about our shared abundance and the plight of the poor—Christians especially. According to a 2017 study by the *Washington Post* and Kaiser Research, Christians are more than twice as likely as non-Christians to associate poverty with a lack of effort as opposed to difficult life circumstances.[6]

Rather than looking at the systemic causes of poverty, more conservative and evangelical followers of Jesus, whose bias for the poor is unmistakable, find comfort in their version of personal piety. Their self-satisfaction assumes that some neighbors in need deserve their circumstances. God said nothing about that to the Hebrews on the Plains of Moab as they received their land of milk and honey. Instead, God expected the opposite—that none should hoard and that all should be provided for.

As it sorts through its great reordering, the church is left to weigh the tension between God's ideas about land, property, and the common good and America's excesses of capitalism, individualism, and exclusive use and ownership.

What's next?

Ministry as Movement: The Church as Sanctuary, Shelter, and Stability

To the local church pastor, leader, volunteer, and disciple, theological claims such as Brueggemann's may seem like admirable but fanciful ideas—laudable but wholly distant and impractical amid the immediate material demands of church congregations and facilities. The sanctuary roof is leaking. The pipe organ moans and groans as if it's dying. Young people don't come to church. The generation that readily made large annual pledges is dying out. The growth of the church triumphant seems to be outpacing the one on earth, at least in America.

Do congregations have the energy to rethink how they use their properties, the creativity to imagine what radical sharing looks like? Do they have the stamina to pull off complex transformation, to take dramatic risks, to think generations ahead, to concern themselves with those we unthinkingly label the "other"? Is it too late to ask these questions? Is God still in charge?

At the apex of twentieth-century American Christendom's influence and power, faithful layman and church critic William Stringfellow observed that the church was preoccupied with religion rather than the gospel. On occasion, however, he said that a congregation would recenter itself on the gospel and recall ministry as an invitation to demonstrate what life after death can look like: "Now and then some Christian risks his life upon the Gospel, and in such events it becomes known in the world that the ministry of Christ lives. At such times, the churches are recalled to that ministry."[7]

How can the church "recall" its ministry? How can it bear witness to God's idea of economic communion? Can it die in order to be reborn? Can it tear itself down to be rebuilt in altogether radical, biblical, and faithful forms?

Those questions will be answered in how the church responds to its upending. Different churches will find new life in different ways. The risky, outlandish notion of building affordable housing on church land has come to dwell in the hearts of a growing movement of congregations. They are reimagining their use of property and, along the way, finding liberation and new identity. On newly defined common ground, they are welcoming the stranger, the sick, the wounded, the impoverished, the oppressed and the outcast into a most intimate relationship.

Crazy by the world's standards, yes, but no crazier than what God has always asked of God's people. They know at least something of what the Israelites felt by following God to the promised land. They have at least a tinge of the wonder the apostles felt when the Spirit first blew through a group of believers who came together and "had all things in common" (Acts 2:44).

As with any movement, many questions remain. Might church property be used for other things that give neighborhoods life and that form and feed community? In many cases, the answer is yes. Building housing on its campus isn't the answer or the call for every congregation. It's reasonable to ask whether churches are really the ones to take up this mission, at least from a practical perspective.

This movement begins only with available land and buildings and, where it can be found, financial capital. So much more is needed to untie the Gordian knot at the heart of the housing crisis—including mental health, social and other support services, political will, and governmental agility. These are big undertakings. Making God's house an actual home requires congregations to muster a new and deeper commitment. These and other matters will be explored in the following chapters.

The consequences—for those needing housing, for those seeking community, and for churches seeking new life—loom large. Clarence Jordan, the Baptist minister/farmer whose faith-based cooperative movement in central Georgia ultimately inspired what became Habitat for Humanity, had experience with such unpopular and sometimes dangerous notions. "Faith," he said, "is not belief in the evidence but a life in scorn of the consequences."[8]

The Stories to Follow: When Death and Resurrection Dance

In the following chapters, we walk with a variety of God's people as they recount their journeys of transformation. Some describe a purely missional call to build housing. Other congregations get close enough to the tomb to take a long look inside and then decide it's time to trust God in altogether new ways.

Just ask the members of Arlington (Virginia) Presbyterian Church outside Washington, DC. In 1908, the people of Arlington Presbyterian put down roots on a piece of open land along a farm lane where horse-drawn buggies shared the road with newfangled horseless carriages. Over time, the church grew in service to what became the Alcova Heights neighborhood of South Arlington. Riding the sweep of American Christianity first up and then down, Arlington Presbyterian held forth and bore witness. It raised generations of children in the faith and sustained a mix of ministries. Despite the integrity of this congregation's witness and the fortitude of its faith, the children grew up and moved away in many cases. Church attendance thinned out. The leaders tired out.

After decades of decline, the congregation decided to take a risk on resurrection. It could have easily sold its valuable property, banked the funds, and limped on. Instead, it leaned into an altogether new kind of legacy. Coordinating through its presbytery (church regional office), it partnered with an affordable-housing developer. Together they imagined new space for the church and its community partners.

As with Westminster Presbyterian Church in Washington, DC, the project at Arlington transformed almost an entire urban block. While the vision was exciting, it came with its share of pain. For long-time members, the buildings held too many memories—so many children's Christmas pageants, so many Easter morning shouts of "Christ is risen," so many baptisms, and so many funerals.

Amid the loss, however, was a stubborn, new hope, says Rev. Ashley Goff, who pastored the congregation into its uncharted future.

"It would have been easy for the congregation to sell its clunky, old property, get $10 million, and ride the wave of decline out," she says. "But the congregation came to realize how inward its focus had become with all the demands of the old building and the old traditions." The journey came with its wilderness period. For more than a year, the congregation met at another church in the neighborhood while the new structure was built. It then waited for the pandemic to wane.

Today the church occupies a far smaller, more flexible worship space centered on the faded copper cross from the church's old steeple. Gone are classrooms, fellowship spaces, the church library, and the official meeting room for the session. The pastor's modest office sits just off the entryway, which also serves as the Sunday morning coffee station. The church has a couple of meeting rooms, one of which doubles as the kids' nursery. In nice weather, the congregation loves to hold gatherings, worship, and other celebrations in a small grove of trees behind the main building.

It's the rest of the property that gives life and mission to the remaining members and neighbors. Alongside the church on the ground floor, a Latino community organization operates a food spot and offers a range of services to immigrant families and others. Above is an apartment building, Gilliam Place, that contains 173 affordable units. "We are in the first generation of the *new* Arlington Presbyterian," Goff says. "We are talking about how we decenter ourselves and focus on our new neighbors. And we are more aware of what we receive in building these new relationships."

Unburdened by the worries of a decaying building and its financial demands, the remnant congregation took a deep breath. It didn't rush in with its own ideas of what its new neighbors "needed." It listened as the residents of the apartments shared their hopes and dreams. Then, in response, the church began offering music lessons to children living in the apartments. It hosted regular community meetings for the surrounding neighborhood as, together, they found their way forward. In God's time, the congregation began to glimpse new possibilities.

"Death and resurrection did a dance in all this, and there was a lot of grieving," says Goff. "Somewhere along the way our people got curious about what was on the other side of death. Now we have the freedom to know God through our neighbor. We aren't tangled up in the stuff that was holding us back. We are not being defined by a certain kind of space and how that space expects us to act, how tradition held us back in that space."

As for the congregation, Arlington's long-term viability is not at all guaranteed. The church has signed a ten-year lease in its new space (the space it used to control). Another honest assessment of the congregation's ongoing vitality will come in the years ahead. For now, however, church members feel free to serve in unexpected ways, and the congregation is unburdened to reimagine its future. When asked what comes next, Goff answers with a wry smile; everything in God's sight, after all, is temporary. "We as a congregation are still vulnerable," she says. "And—spoiler alert—no one gets out of this alive."

For now, though, Goff says, all is new.

Chapter Three

The Church at the Convergence

Crisis, Community, and Call

As author Phyllis Tickle explains in her book *The Great Emergence: How Christianity Is Changing and Why*, every five hundred years or so Christianity goes through "a giant rummage sale" and then starts over.[1] For American Christianity, that cleanout is underway. It poses critical decisions for churches of almost every size, location, and context.

The church I pastor knows those pressures and decisions well. After decades of decline, its members voted to close in 2006. God, however, had a different idea. Caldwell Presbyterian not only remained open but was resurrected. It thrives as a vital, missional, widely diverse, and outwardly focused community of believers and seekers, along with some skeptics and doubters, all looking for God and in pursuit of belonging, meaning, and purpose.

The latest part of Caldwell's rebirth is its transformation of a fourteen-thousand-square-foot campus building to create affordable housing for the chronically homeless. There, at its own convergence of community, call, and Charlotte's housing crisis, the congregation is opening a new chapter in its 114-year story.

That same convergence, facing so many congregations, can be more clearly understood when viewed as a Venn diagram. The illustration below shows the relationship of multiple factors and how they intersect and overlap—and thus where opportunities lie.

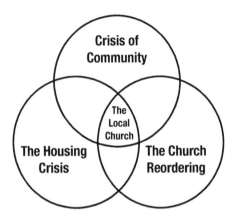

Decades in the making, a housing crisis grips Americans in towns and cities of almost every size and location. Overlapping that crisis is a collapse of community, our failing capacity to form and sustain life together that transcends our increasingly narrow silos of thought, philosophy, worldview, personal history, and experience. The third intersecting factor is more specific to organized religion in America and beyond—one that has reached a tipping point, according to many: the upending of Christianity and the church.

This chapter takes a deeper look at that convergence, beginning with some background on each of the three crises. It follows with an example of how the convergence shaped one church, the one I am blessed to pastor. Caldwell's unexpected journey has called for deep discernment at every milepost. The chapter concludes with some ideas about what we have learned about listening for the Lord.

Crisis #1
The Housing Crisis and How We Got Here

In a nation with deep housing crisis, one of "The Great Ends of the Church" is "The shelter, nurture, and spiritual fellowship of the children of God."[2] In the intersection of those two truths, the church must grapple with its own accountability. This crisis can be seen as a moral failure, a theological calling, a spiritual crisis, or a default by-product of worldly economics. However we look at it, whatever we are doing about the nation's housing crisis, we seem to be forgetting the old adage: "The first step in filling in a hole is to stop digging."

The Hole We've Dug: By the Numbers

The housing crisis shows up in the real lives of its victims—multiple families crammed into a small apartment and those sleeping on a friend's couch, in a shelter, in a tent encampment, under a highway overpass, or in the bushes in a park. The nation's housing crisis takes a human toll that is seen vividly in the numbers:

- Almost one in four renting households pays 50 percent or more of its income for housing, compared to the 30-percent benchmark advised for any household budget.[3]
- Between 2001 and 2021, median rents nationally increased by 17.9 percent, while median household income increased only by 3.2 percent.[4]

As in almost everything, racial disparities compound the inequity and inequality of homeownership. In the fourth quarter of 2021, some 74 percent of white Americans owned a home, compared with 43 percent of Black Americans and 48 percent of Hispanic Americans.[5]

Those at the bottom of the economic ladder bear the heaviest burdens:

- More than 580,000 people experience homelessness on any given night.
- 6.8 million more affordable housing units are needed for families with extremely low incomes.
- 70 percent of all families with extremely low incomes pay more than half their income on rent, forcing daily trade-offs in essential expenses and forestalling any ability to save money.
- 3 out of 4 families with extremely low incomes who need assistance do not receive it.[6]

The pandemic triggered a range of problems that made matters worse. Builders' costs for materials and labor rose, banks tightened lending practices, interest rates rose, and the supply chain sputtered. The number of affordable units needed grew by another 500,000. Extremely low-income renters faced an unmet need for 7.3 million homes. With these combined factors in mind, builders braced for a "production cliff" to hit the market in 2024. "It's the most difficult time I've seen in my thirty years in business, a pretty bleak picture," said Rafael E. Cestero, chief executive of the Community Preservation Corporation, a nonprofit affordable housing financier in New York.[7]

What cost do all Americans pay? There are many ways to add it up. A 2019 study by the U.S. Interagency Council on Homelessness concluded that, for children and adults alike, housing instability or homelessness negatively impacts educational achievement, employment, health, stability, and the preservation of family.[8] Other studies affirm those findings. Especially for the most vulnerable people, housing stability results in better quality of life, reduced trauma symptoms, better mental health, less substance use, fewer arrests, and fewer hospital and emergency room visits.[9]

If you're a dollars-and-cents person, consider these figures:

> Supportive Housing provides significant savings to many public institutions while using no more and sometimes fewer resources in return for better results. For example, in New York, reductions in service use resulted in an annualized savings of $16,282 per unit, which amounts to 95% of the cost of providing supportive housing. In Portland, the annual savings per person amounted to $24,876, whereas the annual cost of housing and services was only $9,870.
>
> A study conducted by the Economic Roundtable in Los Angeles looked at cost savings generated from supportive housing and housing without services. For the general homeless population, temporary or permanent housing (without services) reduces public costs by 50%. But for the chronically homeless, supportive housing reduces public costs by 79% suggesting that adding services gets communities an even greater return for their investment in those that have been homeless the longest.[10]

It took decades to create this crisis, and it will take just as long to reverse it. In the next section, we take a deeper look at the roots of the crisis. For those who like the short version, consider this summary from Pew Research:

> A variety of factors have set the stage for the financial challenges American homeowners and renters have been facing in the housing market, including incomes that haven't kept pace with housing cost increases and a housing construction slowdown. A surge in home buying spurred by record low mortgage interest rates during the COVID-19 pandemic has further strained the availability of homes.[11]

How Did We Get Here?

The roots of our housing crisis run deep.[12] In the closing decades of the nineteenth century, America shifted from a largely agrarian economy to a more industrial one. Millions moved into cities, joined by a wave of immigrants seeking opportunity. This triggered the need for fair, safe, and reasonably priced housing—and ongoing questions about who is responsible for helping ensure all have access to decent shelter.

New York City's Tenement House Act of 1867, the first comprehensive law regulating construction standards, brought some safety and protection. These standards led to later ordinances improving housing for people of color fleeing the Jim Crow South and the subsequent introduction of land use regulations. However, the voices of the property-owning and investor classes were elevated over those of the less well connected. The Great Depression further exposed the vulnerability of the poor as they concentrated even more in urban areas, leading to the establishment of the first public housing policies and properties. While properties were segregated, both white and Black poor people found shelter in them, and the number of public housing units grew.

America's housing supply continued to expand, though it was unjustly and unevenly shared. Local governments in many cities adopted race covenants in new neighborhoods, barring people of color from owning property in what became the most affluent parts of town.

The 1949 U.S. Housing Act expanded homeownership and availability to white returning war veterans, who took advantage of newly established government underwriting for home mortgages. People of color, however, were barred from the so-called American dream by federal and local policies, along with widespread bank redlining. Throughout the twentieth century, white home-owning families built generational wealth while people of color were left to find often substandard rental properties wherever they could, including public housing projects in major metropolitan areas.

The 1956 Interstate Housing Act compounded existing housing disparities. White families followed newly paved roads to the suburbs and often turned their backs on their urban neighbors. Simultaneously, the U.S. Department of Housing and Urban Development launched the profoundly harmful policies of "urban renewal," displacing millions of people of color and disrupting urban communities where Black Americans lived, worshiped, went to school, enjoyed entertainment, and owned businesses. (Chapter 4 describes how policy decisions defined the housing and living patterns in one city, Charlotte, which set the stage for churches to respond with a range of housing options. Chapter 6 explores emerging policy changes that favor church-based housing.)

President Lyndon Johnson secured the passage of the 1965 Fair Housing Act to interrupt redlining and other segregationist housing practices, opening doors to many who had been barred from housing opportunities. But subsequent shifts in the 1970s in housing policy decision-making, from federal to state, including federal "scattered site" housing strategies, advanced the decline in the number of available affordable units.

Federal spending on housing was slashed under the small-government and trickle-down economic theories of the Reagan administration and the neoliberal policies of subsequent administrations, both Democratic and Republican. Budgets for federal housing programs fell from $32 billion in 1981 under the Carter administration to only $4 billion at the end of Ronald Reagan's first term in

1984.[13] A major portion of remaining federal funds was sent to local governments to build housing through private-sector partnerships. In general, though, older units were torn down at a faster pace than new affordable ones were built. In short, through the 1980s, 1990s, and early 2000s, demand for safe and affordable housing went up as supply went down—way down.

The home-building industry slowed to a crawl in the Great Recession in 2008. The COVID-19 pandemic interrupted housing production further as the global supply chain of building materials stalled. Then the COVID recovery superheated the national, state, and local housing markets, driving up the costs of both owner-occupied and rental housing. Harvard University's Joint Center for Housing Studies reported that home price appreciation nationwide hit a thirty-year high in March 2022. What's more, the report noted, the crisis had spread to every corner of the United States: "The runup has been widespread, with 67 of the top 100 housing markets experiencing record-high appreciation rates at some point over the past year. And even in the other 33 major markets, home prices increased by at least 9 percent." Describing the breadth of what it called the "affordability squeeze," the report noted that millions of U.S. households are unable to afford their housing: "Fourteen percent spent more than half of their incomes for shelter. Renters were particularly hard-pressed, with 46 percent at least moderately cost burdened and 24 percent severely burdened."[14] Especially caught in the middle of these shifts of policy and market forces are middle- and lower-income households. A 2022 study by the *New York Times* found "only half of American families living in metro areas can say that their neighborhood income level is within 25 percent of the regional median," down from 62% of families a generation ago.[15] Local zoning ordinances restrict density in development that can bring housing prices down. Meanwhile, without policies encouraging more types of housing, the private sector has been free to chase the upper end of the housing market. In a 2022 article for the *Atlantic*, Jerusalem Demas put it succinctly:

> In a well-functioning market, rising demand for something just means that suppliers will make more of it. But housing markets

have been broken by a policy agenda that seeks to reap the gains of a thriving regional economy while failing to build the infrastructure—housing—necessary to support the people who make that economy go.[16]

Consider the story of Nashville resident Ashley Broadnax. She grew up in the 1990s in a solidly middle-class neighborhood. But, as an adult, the educator, mother, and wife struggled to find an affordable place even reasonably close to her place of employment. "The same people that's working in their city can't afford to live in their city," Broadnax said about Nashville, echoing millions of others in dozens of other cities.[17]

Broadnax's situation shows how deepening housing unaffordability shifted the address of poverty, a process that began after 2000, as documented by the Brookings Institute: "For the first time, suburbs became home to more poor residents than cities," the policy center noted. "Most poor families are working families (roughly two-thirds in both cities and suburbs). . . . A striking share of the poor lives in deep poverty (less than half the federal poverty line) in both cities (46 percent) and suburbs (44 percent)."[18]

The nation's housing crisis is both pervasive and deeply particular for those living a paycheck or a medical crisis away from homelessness. The National Low Income Housing Coalition said in a 2022 report, "The severe shortage of affordable homes for extremely low-income renters is a structural feature of the U.S. housing system, consistently affecting every state and nearly every community, in times of both economic growth and recession. . . . Each of the 50 largest metropolitan areas has a shortage of rental homes affordable and available for renters with household incomes below 50% of [area median income]."Alarmingly, the report called the shortage of affordable homes "a national problem affecting nearly every community." It concluded, "On its own, the private market cannot and will not build and operate homes affordable to extremely low-income families. Only a sustained public commitment can ensure that the lowest-income renters, who are disproportionately people of color, have stable, accessible, and affordable homes."[19]

Crisis #2
A Poverty of Community

The second crisis facing America is a poverty of community. Just as we need a roof over our heads to give us the stability to deal with life's trials and triumphs, God made us as people who also need community to thrive. We are created to be with others—to take on tasks together, to face challenges together, to learn from and rub off on one another, to encourage and affirm one another, to stretch one another, to love one another.

Inside and outside the church, we are people wired to find belonging in the shelter of community, sanctuary to be our best selves. When we go it alone or even in small, homogeneous packs, we fall short of God's purpose for us and our full potential. A proverb widely believed to be of African descent lifts community over individualism: "If you want to go fast, go alone. If you want to go far, go together." Americans and the American church have been going it alone, stalling in our stovepipes, for too long.

About one hundred years after Christ, Irenaeus of Lyon became a bishop. He made his mark, for which he was later sainted in the Catholic tradition, by significantly expanding the Christian movement. As one who saw the Holy Trinity as a community of persons, he famously said, "The glory of God is a living man; and the life of man consists in beholding God."[20]

Irenaeus looked first to God for meaning and purpose. With the community of the Trinity in mind, he understood that meaning and purpose best come in a collective, shared endeavor. We are to reach beyond ourselves and our tribes to know and serve God most fully. Thus, we glorify God not alone but in community.

Not long before his 1968 death, Rev. Dr. Martin Luther King Jr. took time off to write about what was at stake amid the turmoil of the 1960s. America, he wrote, had reached a fork in the road, with one way leading to chaos and the other to community: "In a real sense, all life is interrelated. The agony of the poor impoverishes the rich; the betterment of the poor enriches the rich. We are inevitably our brother's keeper because we are our brother's brother. Whatever affects one affects all indirectly."[21]

King added that the road to true community forsakes the idolatry of putting material things over people. "When machines and computers, profit motives and property rights are considered more important than people, the giant triplets of racism, materialism and militarism are incapable of being conquered."[22] Not only have King's warnings about technology come true, but his "giant triplets of racism, materialism and militarism" have become full-grown adults, thriving in the early twenty-first century more than King could have imagined. Community is their victim.

Personal technology, the prioritization of personal convenience, and the sheer speed of the world all tear at the fabric of togetherness. Of course, technology in specific instances brings tremendous benefits and conveniences. Online calls and meetings kept people and organizations functioning during the pandemic. People living with physical differences can constantly order dinner brought to their door. Many houses of faith now count online worship as standard, and members have come to expect it. Artificial intelligence will transform the economy, bringing benefits but also serious risks.

But technology also quickens our worst isolationist instincts, giving us cover to live unto ourselves as seemingly self-sufficient. We can fool ourselves into thinking we have all the information we need in the palm of our hands, along with self-reinforcing online communities that never disagree with us or invite us to see things differently. Tens of millions of people work from home, sometimes hundreds of miles from their closest coworker. The marketplace develops more and more ways for us to remain isolated or in homogeneous bubbles. This only fuels our loneliness, depression, primal fears of the "other," or our sense that we are in constant competition with others. Good for capitalism. Bad for community. Rather than belonging to God or even to each other, we belong to ourselves. We are our own idols.

Is it too late for the church to reclaim and reassert the vital role of community? Will most Americans continue to wander away from the church to walk their lonely paths of individualistic spirituality? Or can the church build home and community in new ways? Can we reclaim and reinvest in building belonging?

Community builder Peter Block writes that the word *belong* has multiple meanings: "The first is to be related to and be a part of something. . . . Belonging is best created when we join with other people in producing something that makes a place better. It is the opposite of thinking *I must do it on my own.* . . . To belong is to know, even in the middle of the night, that I am among friends." A second meaning, according to Block, has to do with being an owner: "The work, then, is to seek in our own communities a wider and deeper sense of emotional ownership and communal ownership. It means fostering among all of a community's citizens a sense of ownership and accountability, both in their relationships and in what they actually control." Block identifies a third meaning, maybe the most important one for the church: "Belonging can also be thought of as a longing to be. It is the capacity to be present and to discover our authenticity and whole selves. Community is the container within which our longing to be is fulfilled."[23]

For the church and its people, those in the pews now and those who may yet return to church, God calls for more than just any community: God gives us the model of a "beloved community," as Christ illustrated in the Sermon on the Mount and as King echoed in his call to pursue the ideals of love, human dignity, compassion, and equality.

Can God's house reclaim something of that intimate, interdependent, marginalized aspect of the early Jesus movement? Can it become a place where we escape the prisons of our own individualism, where we worship, learn, eat, play, and relax together? Can it become a place where gender expression, race, class, income level, or status matter—because the person with the other experience has something we need to learn? Can the formerly unhoused woman sit in the pew beside a bank executive vice president? Can the trans person sing in the choir alongside the oldest active senior saint, who grew up in the church when Christendom was the center of American life?

Can we build safe places where the voiceless and powerless are centered, heard, valued, and engaged in helping lead what God told Isaiah was coming—"a new thing"? Can we build more churches that are provisional demonstrations of the kindom of heaven in all its diverse, glorious, messy, and lively expressions of our being made in the image of God? Deep down, in such a divided time and nation, aren't we homesick for that kind of place?

Can we make church home again in all the ways people hunger for it—not places where consumers receive services but where a diverse community of faithful stakeholders have passionate coownership of a great undertaking? In finding such a great undertaking, can congregations that are asleep, apathetic, aging, and even dying find new vitality, mission, purpose, faith, and identity?

Can we reclaim what Jesus called koinonia? The essential meaning of koinonia embraces concepts conveyed in the English terms "community," "communion," "joint participation," "sharing" and "intimacy."[24] Can we recreate the jointly contributed gift of community and communion, extending all the gifts we have from "the giver of all good things"?

All types of institutions—but particularly the church—must answer these questions, according to theologian Willie James Jennings. He asserts that it is the primary job of the Christian community to use all its resources to close gaps rather than open them:

> At the heart of Christian community is the call to create belonging where there had been boundary, border, separation and segregation. A Christian sense of belonging always cuts across every other kind of alignment and allegiance. . . . A sense that what happens in this place, this city, this town, this community matters to me. What happens in this place affects me. In order to make that kind of ethic clear, we have to work against alienation, displacement. We have to work against the logic of private property that tells us that what happens on my land is my business and nobody else's.[25]

So what *is* happening on church land in the first part of the twenty-first century?

A Poverty of Missional Imagination?

The numbing narrative in too many congregations is that "the church is dying." It's undeniable that the church is changing dramatically. God the midwife is at the bedside, and we are feeling the sharp pangs of labor. The data can be overwhelming:

- Twenty percent of Americans attend church every week, forty one percent attend monthly or more and fifty seven percent seldom or never attend worship, according to Gallup.[26]
- On any given weekend, about three in ten U.S. adults attend religious services, down from 42 percent two decades ago. "Church attendance will likely continue to decline in the future, given younger Americans' weaker attachments to religion."[27]
- "Specifically, more 18- to 29-year-olds, 35%, say they have no religious preference than identify with any specific faith, such as Protestant/nondenominational Christian (32%) or Catholic (19%). Additionally, young adults, both those with and without a religious preference, are much less likely to attend religious services—22% attend regularly, eight points below the national average."[28]
- When adjusted for inflation, average congregational costs in the Presbyterian Church (U.S.A.) are $54,620 higher than the average church income, pointing to a gap that churches everywhere are feeling.[29]

The largest-ever congregational study, the 2020 Faith Communities Today report by the Hartford Institute for Religion Research, noted, "The research is clear that this moment demands real change if a large percentage of faith communities are to survive the next 20 years with spiritual vibrancy and ministry effectiveness."[30]

An even starker perspective, that as many as one in three churches could close in the years to come, comes from a professional organization grappling with the housing crisis and looking for its own answers. According to the International City/County Management Association, "In the aftermath of the current public health crisis, the number of church closings will increase dramatically. Conservatively, the number will double or triple."[31]

Hard facts? Yes. These hard truths could trigger either resignation or resilience and re-creation. Whatever the reasons for the decline—and that is neither my expertise nor focus—we are still Easter people, are we not? People of the resurrection? People who believe that even death as we may think of it did not, and does not, get the final word?

Communities of Faith

Maybe the way back to community is for us to change our perspective and our expectations of one another and of organized religion. As people of faith, we have a God who created all things, who is best known in the lived and risen Christ, and who dances in our midst in the impossibly unpredictable wildness of the Holy Spirit.

But the church, it seems, has forgotten how to dance. It has become what organizational consultants call a "stuck" organization, mired in bad habits and negative language. As an alternative, Peter Block prescribes valuing possibility and relatedness over problems, needs, self-interest, and the rest of the stuck community's agenda: "Shifting the context from retribution to restoration will occur through the use of language that moves in the following directions: from problems to possibility; from fear and fault to gifts, generosity and abundance; from law and oversight to social capital and chosen accountability; from the dominance of corporation and systems to the centrality of associational life; from leaders to citizens."[32]

Somewhere along the way, the church has failed to convey God's love, meaning, purpose, and calling as good news—desperately needed, ultimately satisfying, and all sufficient. Somewhere we took a back seat to other, louder voices and, of late, voices of sheer meanness and fear. In the largesse of the church's heyday, in the middle of what is called "the American Century," when Christianity was the norm, perhaps the church got lazy, self-satisfied, and complacent. We lost our agility and passion, our sense that we are a bottom-up movement rather than a top-down institution.

Perhaps, even, we took God's promise in Christ for granted. We got drunk on our abundance. We forgot that God's grace, while unmerited, is demanding and costly in that curious way of God's economy. Perhaps we grew unaccountable in our response to grace. Interestingly, in an era when progressive and conservative Christians agree on little, the call to "redo" church spans the ideological wings of the church. Rev. Lenny Duncan offers his own strong medicine— if we can take it. He is a Lutheran pastor who hardly fits the role as dictated by central casting—a person of color in a vastly white denomination, a member of the LGBTQ community, an outsider on the inside and, most of all, someone who loves God and the church desperately. He writes, "Our communities have bought into the idea that 'church is dying,' so anything that could upset the status quo is seen as dangerous, subversive, and unchristian. Christianity at its core is subversive."[33] Duncan insists that the church is not dying but being refined like a precious metal even through our fear and anxiety.[34] With his passion comes honesty, too, about the work and days ahead—if we are to reclaim the promise of being "fully alive" together in community. Writing to the church, he continues: "You are the generation that has been chosen for this time, this place, this moment in human history.[35]

A New Openness in an Old Place: Caldwell Presbyterian Church

Lenny Duncan's honesty can sound plenty daunting. You may stop reading right here. I get it. Every week, long-declining churches that perceive no future make the decision to spend down what's left in the bank and seek a gracious closure.

What the church needs badly is a new openness. Many denominations may feel restrained or even paralyzed by the rules and regulations of their ecclesial polity and policy. For example, in the Presbyterian Church (U.S.A.) where I am an ordained minister, many understandably squirm under our denomination's reputation for doing everything "decently and in order" (1 Cor. 14:40). But even our *Book of Order* offers a needed word for these times of change and reconstruction: "In Jesus Christ, who is Lord of all creation, the Church seeks a new openness to God's mission in the world."[36]

I will be forever grateful for the "new openness" demonstrated by the stalwart, octogenarian Calvinists at what was Caldwell Memorial Presbyterian Church in Charlotte. Their journey from prosperity to scarcity and then to a new kind of abundance reflects that of many churches caught in the polycrisis—a neighborhood swept up on the changing currents of a fast-growing city, an implosion of community, and a lack of bold vision. Their resurrection from near death is a testament to God's dancing Spirit of renewal, hope, and possibility.

A Promising Start Met by Familiar Challenges

In a city with a deep Presbyterian heritage, the church opened in 1912 on the edge of Charlotte as it hit one of its many growth spurts. At the heart of one of the city's first two suburbs beyond its central core, the congregation grew as the new area of town developed. It counted 500 members by the 1920s and, by the late 1950s, 1,100 members, the apex of its membership. In its prime, Caldwell looked like a lot of mainstream Protestant congregations. Ministers preached the tenets of Calvinism. Children attended Sunday school and sang in age-staged choirs. The women of the church met with their concerns while the men focused mostly in finances, foreign mission, and doing all things decently and in order.

In the 1960s and 1970s, as with many inner-city, historic neighborhoods, suburban sprawl vacuumed people out of Caldwell's surrounding, historic Elizabeth neighborhood to newer, bigger houses, broader lawns, and shinier, new Presbyterian churches. Many of the gracious homes were chopped up into apartments, and the neighborhood took on a funky flair of mixed-income folk. (Caldwell, as with most Presbyterian churches, had only ever been a white, middle-class congregation, somewhat conservative in its theology and traditional in its mission.)

Over time, membership began to fall, and it fell and fell and fell some more. At the cusp of the twenty-first century, Rev. Dr. Charles (Charlie) MacDonald was assigned as temporary interim pastor, charged to determine whether the church had any future at all. He was the right person for the job. Having served affluent, cathedral-style Presbyterian churches in Detroit as well as small, triracial churches in the back hills of Virginia, Charlie had seen it all.

Trained as an engineer, Charlie blended a powerful intellect and an unshakable sense of biblical justice. During the years of racial integration, he served a church in Virginia that debated whether to seat Black folks who came to worship. In a meeting, a vociferous member declared, "They shall not be seated in our sanctuary." In his characteristic, calm way, Charlie replied, "Fine. Then I will move worship to the parking lot." In Caldwell's hope for resurrection, he was the right man for the job.

When Charlie arrived at Caldwell after a string of other pastors, the remaining, aging members drew one more deep breath and rallied again. At first, the remnant congregation held out hope. But it became clear in short order that Caldwell had lost too much momentum. By the fall of 2006, worship attendance was down to about twelve active members, and three aging elders made up the session; with no endowment and its reserves drained by decades of decline, the church couldn't even afford to keep the lights on and to pay two meager, part-time salaries.

The few who had remained voted to close the church. That's when the Holy Spirit swept over the church with a new possibility and, indeed, a new openness. On the Sunday when the vote to close the church was announced, a young couple that had been visiting was in the pews. They were part of a small, independent group of believers and seekers that had weeks before begun renting a room on Sunday nights for study and community.

Meeting under the name the Agape Group, they had been part of a rare, diverse, missional, inclusive, koinonia-like congregation, Seigle Avenue Presbyterian Church, a couple of miles away. That congregation modeled what social justice–centered discipleship looked like in a city full of lovingly, frozen-chosen, tall-steeple Presbyterian and other churches.[37]

In its last decades, however, Seigle Avenue Presbyterian was not financially self-sufficient. As important as its inner-city work was, it was a mission church funded significantly by an across-town, affluent, tall-steeple congregation. Seigle's diversity added to its fragility, as differences in race, class, and life experience sometimes fueled misunderstanding and conflict. Finally, it splintered. For several years, dozens of its members sought another church like it but couldn't find one. While some found new church homes, many remained out of church altogether.

A Seed Takes Root

The Agape Group that had begun meeting at Caldwell had no particular plans for its future. Its members enjoyed gathering on Sunday nights; there was no official pastoral leadership, just eating together, studying the Word, seeking ways to serve. In a word, they craved community. Among them were Tovi and Kevin Martin, who began to attend worship occasionally at Caldwell on Sunday mornings. The Martins came to value Charlie's wise, unpretentious preaching. As a mixed-race couple, they felt authentic welcome from the tiny, senior remnant of membership in the mostly empty sanctuary. When the Martins approached Charlie on the day he announced Caldwell would close, they inquired how they might help. "Do you have any friends?" Charlie asked.

Two weeks later, the Agape Group and a few friends came to worship. Serving as an usher that day was Jimmy Todd. A successful entrepreneur, retired and in his seventies, he had grown up at Caldwell and had fought hard to keep Caldwell open. As he stood at the main door to the church, he watched the newcomers stream in—young and old, Black and white, some in coats and ties, others in slacks and T-shirts, doctors, professors and teachers, managers of nonprofit organizations, and aging social justice warriors. Jimmy and the rest of the remnant congregation extended a warm, joyous welcome to the visitors.

"There were so many of them and only one of me. I figured I'd better be the one to do the changing," Jimmy said in an interview about those days.

Charlie MacDonald called the presbytery to report that there had been a change in plan and that he would not be surrendering the keys to the church, at least not right away. Slowly, Charlie blended the newcomers with the stalwart remnant, whose new openness made a place for the arrivals' new energy and passion.

A few months later, on Easter morning 2007, the *Charlotte Observer* featured the unlikely church resurrection as the feature, front-page story under the banner headline "The Miracle on 5th Street." In the following weeks of Eastertide, the congregation lived into the promise of 2 Corinthians 5:17 that in Christ the old had passed away and had been made new in ways no one could have expected. Members studied Scripture through old and new perspectives but always found "true north" by looking at Christ's life-giving lessons of compassion, inclusivity, and justice-loving. Embracing the liberation of a new beginning, the congregation met over several weeks to craft a new mission statement:

> We seek to build a diverse, intentional, affirming community animated by joyful worship and called forth into social action for service to the greater good.
>
> We seek to hear God's call not only as individuals but also as a progressive, missional community striving to reflect the Kingdom of God in the here and now.
>
> We embrace the rich history of the Reformed Tradition and the storied past of our center-city church, as we welcome a diverse community of seekers—ALL ages, races and ethnicities, sexual orientations, cultural and economic backgrounds, gender identities, and family structures—ALL people.
>
> We are called into a meaningful, transformative community that values the unique blessings and perspectives of each member and offers a place of welcome and healing to weary souls.
>
> We seek dynamic servant leaders who serve humbly, embrace change, and boldly challenge injustices in the wider community. Most importantly, we seek to proclaim the Gospel in both word and deed, following the life and teachings of Jesus Christ, our Lord and Savior.

The unexpected resurrection of Caldwell Church wasn't always pretty, but it was always an adventure. In time, an intersectional congregation formed made up of a mix of races, religious and faith backgrounds, sexual orientations, identities, economic classes, and life stages.

Charlie MacDonald recognized the new future taking shape for Caldwell—and how much work it would require. At age seventy-eight, he breathed a sigh of relief and signaled his retirement. He thanked God that his long, varied, and accomplished ministerial career would end in such a meaningful but unexpected way.

A Spiritual Hospital for the Wounded and Weary

After leaving the private sector, finishing seminary, and being approved for a call, I'd come alongside Charlie as a volunteer assistant. A newly minted rookie, I was happy to have the experience. For a year, I was both a banker for forty hours a week and a volunteer for another twenty. In the spring of 2008, the congregation formally called me to serve as the ordained pastor.

The renewal rolled on. Its progressive, social justice–oriented mission and theology found a following. Its worship style remained familiar to longtime Presbyterians and other Protestants, but it was more relaxed and even joyful. Caldwell became a "destination church," attracting people from twenty-five zip codes, four counties, and two states across the Charlotte region. It was also a safe haven for many who had become disillusioned by organized religion, been wounded elsewhere by church, or given up on organized religion for other reasons.[38]

Caldwell grew, built up some financial stability, and began sharing its ample campus space with a range of mission partners and other community organizations. The congregation felt strongly that its second chance amounted to a divine mandate to share its space openly as a demonstration of the same kind of radical welcome all the newcomers had felt. Through various connections, human and divine, the church came to house a bilingual preschool for children of the area's fast-growing Latino population; two public education-focused nonprofit agencies; a mental-health counseling agency; and a Black sister church that worshiped on our campus on Sunday afternoons for two years. Caldwell later opened a nonprofit coffee shop to train youth for job readiness. In each case, God and the Spirit led to these relationships. As these campus partners shared our spaces, the church stretched and grew, struggled, learned, and came away deeply blessed and renewed, if not at times a little tired. Experimentation and risk-taking, never exactly reckless but often daring at the very least, became an important part of the congregation's DNA.

Where Next, O Lord? Discernment and Decision

A few years into its new life, Caldwell celebrated its centennial, confident and faithful enough to claim a second century for the unlikely flock. Members took a year to pray, study, listen, and discern what God was calling the church to do. It named a team of leaders to guide and facilitate a season of deep discernment—listening to the cries of our city and the many passions of our diverse flock, taking stock of what we had learned since the church's resurrection and what we thought we had to offer.

Such moments of decision come for most every church—multiple times in most congregations. It is easy and understandable to avoid them, however. The longer we go without them, the more hardened our arteries become and the more sacred our pet cows grow. Our spaces become just that—*our* spaces, only to be offered to others on certain terms and conditions, if at all. "Our kind of worship" becomes *the only* way to worship, our music the only kind of church music, our mission the only kind of mission.

Putting all that on the table takes faith, courage, and thick skin. Powerful personalities—including big pledgers—are often involved. Too frequently, the pastor or other staff members are stuck with the task of asking the risky question or pointing out the elephant in the room. *Members must lead courageously.* When big questions get raised, pastors are often burned out or walking on eggshells. Sooner or later every pastor hears the illustrative story about the longtime, multi-generational family who greets the new pastor upon arrival. Then, before long, the family reminds the pastor, subtly or not so, that while pastors have always come and gone, their family holds the keys to the church. (I don't recall hearing about those families in the Scriptures, but I do remember that Moses struggled with the stiff-necked Israelites and Christ had to deal with the Pharisees.)

Congregations also have a right to ask how much risk is too much risk. Members pour their sweat and blood into a place and become protective, forgetting it was God's to begin with. Many Christians are not risk-takers by habit, even though much of our heritage is rooted in people who were chased out of their home country and had to start with little to nothing.

Still, we are not just *permitted* to take risk, to embrace a new openness. We are *commanded* to follow the head of the church, Jesus Christ. He knew a few things about taking risks for the sake of the gospel. How often do we speak about the call to be more effective in our mission by being more open to new callings and new seasons, new ideas about worship and what some may call "risky" uses of our church properties? How often do we shrink from the baptismal proposition that to have new life we have to die to our old selves, our old ways, our fears and hesitancy?

Flinging Open the Doors, Throwing Spaghetti on the Wall

The "new" Caldwell flock looked to the example of the original members, who opened the church doors and their hearts to God's undying promise to do a "new thing." They held the gift God had given in their hands gently and respectfully. They also didn't mind throwing spaghetti on the wall to see what might stick in the way of new, sometimes nutty ideas. They knew their century-old buildings were sturdy and that a wet noodle stain could be wiped off. They believed God must have saved the church to do new things.

Throughout 2013, meeting regularly, opening the floor to all, and making lists on big notepads on the wall, members captured every idea that was voiced—all sixty-eight. They sought to value each voice and idea, so no one felt left out or cast aside. They sorted the ideas by size and scale. Some were big, audacious (and sometimes a little scary) dreams: launch a ministry to the neighboring community, launch a faith-based social enterprise, start an after-school program for at-risk kids at the elementary school across the street. Other ideas, such as tweaking the order of worship, were "just do its." The biggest ideas all had to do with the possibilities of the aging but spacious buildings on a 1.3-acre lot in a thriving, historic neighborhood within walking distance of the center-city business district.

In its prime, life at Caldwell centered not just on the sanctuary but on its fourteen-thousand-square-foot Price Education Building.[39] Generations flowed through its halls—adult Sunday school classes supported each other through life's ups and downs, youth learned catechisms, and babies overflowed the nursery. But that was at the height of twentieth-century American Christianity. For the "new" Caldwell, its "Christian education building" became a kind of mission laboratory, incubating and housing a range of community partners.

It was still an "education building," but it provided a different kind of missional formation.

In the midst of the Great Recession, the congregation saw the Spirit moving again, redirecting its attention to the hundreds of tired, vulnerable, and unhoused women caught in a city that had provided adequate shelter beds for single men and for women with children but not enough beds for single women. The Salvation Army asked Caldwell if it would offer its education building as a temporary shelter while more permanent space could be built. Caldwell might have hesitated or stopped right there. It might have convinced itself that the risks and unknowns were too many, too daunting. But the congregation focused on the women on the streets and said yes.

"The ladies," as they became known to us, were not the only ones to move in. So did the Holy Spirit. What was to be an emergency shelter for only sixty days grew into a three-and-a-half-year relational ministry that changed our members. The congregation cooked and served a hot breakfast on Sundays and launched a range of offerings for the weeknights, from computer skills to job interviewing, from yoga to sewing, from "dress for success" parties to arts-and-crafts fun to beauty shows. Some of the ladies joined the church.

The impromptu shelter did bring operational headaches and challenges. It called on everyone's patience and grace—a lot. Some days were harder than others. But on the whole, Caldwell loved it. More importantly, our hearts changed as did our understanding of life on the streets in a city that was busy moving forward without always taking care of all its citizens.

Coming to Grips with Charlotte's Housing Crisis

Eventually the Salvation Army completed construction on the expansion at its main shelter facility. The ladies moved out. Caldwell caught its breath. That was about the time of its postcentennial year of discernment. The congregation generated that list of sixty-eight ideas of what it wanted to do in its second century. And members realized they were grieving the absence of our guests and the opportunity to offer them not just shelter but a sense of belonging. We missed the enriched sense of community that the shelter had given us for those years.

The congregation increased its focus on housing its neighbors in other ways. It spent a year studying why, in the nation's second-largest banking center, more than three thousand people were on the street each night and tens of thousands of others lived at risk of becoming homeless. Members looked closely at the factors behind the problem. They probed the experience of never knowing where one might sleep or get the next meal. They asked why the unhoused lacked the stability they needed to focus on the root causes of their homelessness.

Caldwell measured its own assets—financial, human, physical, and spiritual. The consensus was clear. Caldwell would dedicate the Price Building for the foreseeable future to address the city's housing crisis. It would follow the example of the Samaritan Jesus spoke of in the Gospel of Luke, whose gut-rending compassion for the beaten and abandoned traveler moved him to care for and shelter the traveler until he was better. The church zeroed in on a call to house the chronically homeless—those with 30 to 50 percent of the area median income. The church chose a "housing first" model, which would serve mostly people coming off the streets with the existing challenges often found amid poverty—addiction, mental health challenges, and other needs. But the church knew that all were children of God.

The vision demanded years of work. By the fall of 2022, Caldwell members had returned to worship and active church life from the interruptions of the COVID-19 pandemic. As members returned home to church, the congregation scheduled a celebration to launch the new housing initiative. We gathered in the vacant Price Building, where a target symbol had been drawn on one of the entryway plaster walls. Red-headed Evan Ashley, age six, took the first swing with a mini-sledgehammer to break open not just the wall but a new future for many. In a century-old building once jammed with Sunday school attendees, Caldwell's more hands-on form of Christian education took another step forward. More about what is now called Easter's Home comes in later chapters.

Principles of Discernment: The Importance of the How and the What

Every church finds itself in seasons of discernment. They don't always go neatly. Along the way at Caldwell, we had some disagreements and healing conversations. What the congregation did most was trust God, the God who for some reason had not wanted Caldwell to close a few years earlier.

We still draw from the deep well of trust and faith we dug in those days as we move forward with our housing initiative. We have our share of unknowns and anxiety about the complexities of what we are doing. But God is always there as we grow and learn, and our memories of our years with "the ladies" remind us how the Lord has a way of working things out in surprising ways. Step-by-step we try to turn the unknowns into knowns, and we trust the Lord with the unknowables.

Whether a church is considering the anything-but-easy call to provide housing on its campus or another mission calling, the "how" of the congregational conversation proves every bit as important as the "what" of the outcome. Building congregational consensus at each step, including and listening to as many voices as possible, is essential to finishing the journey. Conversely, failing to do so is more than likely to create problems down the road.

Most important to our process was trusting that God would provide guidance and direction—and equip our members with practices of mutual respect and forbearance, a radical openness to any notion or possibility, patience to wait on God to move, and humility in understanding that there is always more to be learned. A few key principles of any deep process of discernment (expanded in appendix B) include:

- Pray in everything!
- Consider your church's history in its neighborhood or community.
- Define a pathway for the process the congregation will follow, including labeling as many steps as possible, on the front end.
- Communicate, communicate, communicate. Transparency in everything will build trust and buy-in.

- Try to identify what you don't know, and bring in experts.
- Listen more than talk.
- Engage those who express skepticism or disagreement with the emerging vision.
- Value the opinions of all, regardless of their financial capacity or the length of time they have been involved with the church.
- Model grace, and ask for it from all—but know that it won't always show up.
- Center the voice of the other and the newcomer.
- Use a diverse and representative set of people to lead the listening.
- If you can, recruit a third-party facilitator.
- And pray without ceasing!

Stories from the Church Housing Movement

Seasons of discernment come at different times for different churches, and each congregation has its context and considerations. Sometimes change comes from within. Other times it is forced on a church. In 2020, however, every church shared one common experience—enduring the pandemic. By necessity, churches adapted to offering ministry that depended less on buildings and grounds and more on relationships. In his role as general presbyter (the top regional executive) for the Washington, DC, region of the Presbyterian Church (U.S.A.), Rev. John Molina-Moore has seen how congregations have begun to think differently. "Some people have gone decades without seeing the church in a new way," he says. "The pandemic showed them how to be more relational. Now they are more ready to think about what building housing will require."

Two congregations in his presbytery called new pastors to lead them with realizing housing-specific dreams. Their dreams cost them some families who disagreed and decided to leave. In other congregations, plans to build housing have attracted new members who are excited to be part of the new venture. In one congregation, stewardship giving has increased since a plan was announced to house the church's neighbors. "They see that there is something on the horizon that is different from a slow and painful march toward closure," Molina-Moore says. "They see a new light at the end of the tunnel."

For Caldwell, the vision that emerged was to create twenty-one permanent supportive-housing studio apartments for those who had experienced chronic homelessness. But that is only one option for housing. In the following chapter, we hear from churches that felt called to build housing for other segments of the population with different needs.

This movement is just beginning, and these stories are from the front lines of learning. From almost every one of the cases I have studied, including my conversations with leaders and partners, I'm convinced that God is up to something powerful. In many cases these congregations have found new freedom, liberation, and identity in mission in building the beloved community in many forms.

As we turn to their stories and voices, let us listen first to the prayer of the small but faithful flock of Church of the Resurrection in Arlington, Virginia, as they prepared to tear their church down to make way for new possibilities:

> Our loving God, thank you for giving us a mission and the heart to do what you ask. Please keep us together as a church to carry out this offering of love and to continue serving others in your name. We give you our fear, for you are our guide.

Chapter Four

One City's Confluence

Charlotte's Housing Crisis and the Call to (Re)Build Community

Each city and town has its own story—its own version of how it came to be and how its people came to live together or apart. Each of those stories is woven out of its own regional and cultural distinctions, social factors, economic features, racial truths, and religious narratives. In each case, some truths are lifted up, some are buried, and some are erased. Some are confessed, and others are kept silent. Each also has its version of the polycrisis that is the focus of this book—the convergence of declining community; the growing number of churches at important, if not existential, crossroads; and a shortage of safe, affordable, and dignified places to live.

This chapter traces how one city—Charlotte, North Carolina— came to be. Charlotte is thriving by many measures. As one of the fastest-growing cities in America (the fifteenth-fastest in 2022),[1] Charlotte welcomes as many as one hundred new residents a day according to some studies. But by other measures, Charlotte excludes people just as rapidly. Charlotte also has its home-grown version of the nation's deepening gap between the haves and have-nots. In 2019–2023, its number of homes valued at $1 million or more grew 142 percent to 17,000, while its number of unsheltered people rose 35 percent.[2] The rich got richer and the poor poorer.

How did we get here? This chapter looks briefly at how Charlotte's history shaped its neighborhoods and people patterns. We then look at the city's churches that have or are building affordable housing on their properties in response to the city's housing crisis. As it turns out, Charlotte is something of a pacesetter in this movement. That's good because there is a lot of work to do and harm to repair.

Charlotte's housing mistakes are captured in two looming legacies. One is of long-lasting segregation and latter forms of separation, rooted in white supremacy. Charlotte's second legacy is one of displacement of people of color. These legacies bear important lessons. They also frame what some churches are doing to address the city's housing crisis.

In describing the city's housing and development patterns, local historian Tom Hanchett depicts today's Charlotte as a city of "sectors," resembling a pie cut into slices.[3] These outcomes reflect the influence of developers far more than any sustained, discernible plan or strategy. We are divided by race and class—in how we live and in how we know each other. It was not always that way. It might have turned out differently.

The Making of a City: Mapping
Its Milestones and Mistakes

What we now call the Carolinas was, of course, already occupied when the first "settlers" came to the piedmont region. For centuries, the Catawba, Sugaw, and Waxhaw indigenous peoples lived here, hunting and practicing their ways of commerce and trading. The very heart of what is now Charlotte was the intersection of two ancient trading paths.

When the colonials came, they gave their own names to those intersecting trading paths. One was dubbed Trade Street, appropriate for the city's future identity as an ever-burgeoning business hub. They named the other path Tryon Street to honor the British colonial governor who sponsored the settlement. In many ways, the heart of Charlotte is still the intersection of commerce and power.

For decades, Charlotte was a quiet place of a few merchants and tradesmen that grew at a rather unremarkable rate. Upon passing through the town, George Washington called it "a trifling place." The Revolutionary War swept around it.[4] Originally the townspeople built homes and settled in what Hanchett terms "a salt-and-pepper" pattern. It mixed races and classes in a grid pattern of streets that, over time, grew out from the intersection of Trade and Tryon. Charlotte's growth and economic prowess increased as the south embraced King Cotton and slavery. Planters and other investors soon established a rail line to move their crops to other markets and ports, giving rise to one of the city's economic cornerstones—transportation. Along came professions to support and facilitate expanding trade—finance, law, merchandise, and others.

Charlotte was spared the destruction from the Civil War that set back other Southern cities, allowing it to recover economically more quickly. By the turn of the nineteenth century, textile mills opened and, with them, mill villages that began to expand the city limits. Over time, the area's economy became more industrialized than agrarian, bringing more residents to the city, both white and Black. The city's population in 1880 was 47 percent Black, 53 percent white.

Through the ensuing decades, Charlotte emerged as a business town, demonstrating success, ingenuity, and enterprise. One economic wave followed another, driven by enterprise and energy more than natural resources or geographic advantage. Toward the close of the twentieth century, Charlotte took its place alongside New York and San Francisco as one of the nation's three largest banking centers. It welcomed professional sports franchises, nicer restaurants, high-rent condo towers, and more corporate headquarters—outpacing its mid-size Southern peer cities and bringing it the national attention it had long sought as Atlanta's smaller cousin.

The Great Recession of 2008 and the COVID-19 pandemic only paused the city's steady and sometimes overheated growth. Soon it was booming again, adding technology and health care to its upper-income job base and attracting ongoing streams of newcomers. Many came from bigger, more expensive cities in the Northeast and California, attracted by Charlotte's pleasant climate and more manageable size. With them came inflated housing demand and prices.

But it all came with a cost that isn't borne evenly. Charlotte is a victim of its own success. The service and hospitality workers the city depends on—those who prepare and serve food, trim yards, and clean houses, hospitals, and hotel rooms—cannot afford to live in the city. If they do, they are doubling and tripling up on how many dwell in a single home or apartment. A growing number must live in outlying towns and counties.

All this exposes how the city's housing and real estate development patterns and practices continue to be shaped by decades-old politics and policies meant to segregate neighborhoods by race and class. In specific, two legacies stand tall.

A Legacy of Separation

If given the chance to step back in time to the 1890s, we would glimpse a Charlotte that might have been. The city was growing in industry, transportation, commerce, and population. It also faced new questions of how to shape its neighborhoods and how its residents would live together.

A quarter century after the end of slavery, there was a moment when the interests of the middle- and lower-income working classes, Black and white, came together in what is known as Fusion politics. The movement began to create political power that took interest in housing and working conditions, among other topics.

Just as quickly, though, moneyed, white interests put the movement down. Using the city's leading newspaper and other means to spread racist fear and rumors, white supremacists in the city took back power in the 1898 election. In the opening decades of the new century, Jim Crow settled in comfortably, and the city's brief chance at a fair and equitable future passed almost as quickly as it had appeared.[5]

While quoting the ordinance language, Hanchett writes that when Charlotte opened its first "suburban" public recreation ground, the spacious Independence Park, "the Board of Alderman passed an ordinance specifying that 'no colored person shall be allowed except as nurses to white children.'"[6] Real estate developers picked up on the practice. The developer of the Piedmont Park neighborhood (now part of the Elizabeth area of town) introduced the practice of race-restricted deeds for home lots, stipulating the price of homes that could be built and that none could be owned "by any person of the Negro race."[7]

The real estate development patterns set in the early 1900s continued to govern Charlotte's residential spread. In time, the racial deed restrictions that defined early neighborhoods, such as Piedmont Park (Elizabeth) and Myers Park, were lifted. Real estate developers resorted to marketing tactics that continued to steer Black buyers to some neighborhoods and whites to others. Overall, white and affluent residents owned homes and Black families lived in rental housing in more depressed areas. Other equally insidious factors followed and extended the city's segregated housing patterns: bank redlining, the exclusion of Black veterans from the GI bill, and discriminatory rental practices.[8] Federally funded programs of the mid to latter decades of the twentieth century created public housing, concentrating residents by race and income level.

Today, as in many metros where legalized segregation and other white-privileged housing policies once ruled the day, there are two cities, two Charlottes. If you examine a map of population by race, Charlotte's legacy of separation stands out. The mostly white, affluent area began in neighborhoods with racial covenants. It spills to the southeast out from the center city as one suburb of quarter- and half-acre lots and two-story homes connecting to the next. What locals sometimes call "the wedge" now extends to the South Carolina state line and beyond.

To the north and west of the center city, what some call "the crescent," is an arc of lower-income, largely Black neighborhoods. Just as the affluent area began with neighborhoods that were race-restricted, many of the poorer, Black neighborhoods connect back to another important legacy—the Brooklyn community.

A Legacy of Displacement

For a time, Charlotte's Black citizens had a place of their own—not so much of their choosing but by necessity. Residents called it Brooklyn, an homage to the thriving, Black borough of New York City. Its destruction in the 1960s at the hands of the city's white power brokers—absent any input from Black leaders or citizens—gutted the city's Black community. As if a bomb was dropped on one quarter of the center city, the explosion of this community still ripples across the city. The families and descendants of Brooklyn's former residents still search for safe and affordable places to live in today's

Charlotte. Many of them worship in the same Black churches that are building affordable housing today. Brooklyn's legacy still speaks, and these churches are responding.

How did it all happen? By the 1880s, Reconstruction had given Black Charlotte residents reason for hope. Attracted by available land and affordable rentals, many Black families gathered in Second Ward, the city's southeast quadrant. The brief success of the Fusion political movement coalesced political interests across racial lines in the 1890s. As it drew the backlash of white supremacy, the movement died, and racial division deepened as the city's norm.

However, Charlotte's Black residents built what they needed in the Brooklyn community, which filled one of the city's four central wards and spanned about fifty blocks. In time, the community grew into a town within a town. It provided whatever its residents could want, from cradle to grave: schools, churches, theaters, night clubs, civic clubs, barber shops, doctors' offices, beauty parlors, and funeral homes.[9]

Brooklyn's housing stock reflected the full range of its residents' circumstances, from smaller shanties to the fine homes of some of the city's most accomplished Black families. Cars traveled a mix of paved streets and dirt roads, which was all the city government had built in some of Brooklyn's low-lying, flood-prone land.

In Brooklyn's business district, the AME Zion Publishing House produced church resources sent to the African Methodist Episcopal Church Zion's three million members around the world. Founded in 1922 by some of the city's most prominent and accomplished Black professionals, the Mecklenburg Investment Company attracted Black doctors, lawyers, and business owners to the city and provided seed capital to new Black enterprises. The African-American Insurance Company sold policies across the state. Black leaders of businesses, schools, and churches organized and spoke up for their neighbors. And it was all Black-owned and Black-run. "Charlotte's Brooklyn was a living, breathing example of Black brilliance and resilience in the heart of the Jim Crow South," writes Greg Jarrell in his penetrating analysis of Brooklyn's full history. "It was bakers and mechanics and undertakers and musicians, holidays and funeral processions and struggle and triumph."[10] But it was not to last, and a racially charged attack on housing rooted in white supremacy brought it all down. By the 1930s and '40s, federal housing programs helped create neighborhoods on the city's west side that were marketed to the few Black families who could afford to buy. In Brooklyn, meanwhile, much of the white-owned rental housing stock was left to fall into disrepair and neglect.

The city of Charlotte destroyed Brooklyn's Black communities with labels that would "qualify" the city for sizable federal grants. These monies served its commercial needs but, by a long shot, not the needs of all the people. In 1947, Charlotte passed a comprehensive zoning overhaul, labeling most of Brooklyn's land as "industrial," a precursor to the sweeping federal program of "urban renewal" that changed the face of cities across the nation in the name of "improvement and progress."

In 1958, the city government labeled most of Brooklyn "blighted." That official designation helped qualify the city for $1.4 million in new federal grants made available to "renew" urban neighborhoods. Black leaders appealed, saying in part that the city had built no affordable public housing for its low-income families in Brooklyn. The NAACP protested that no Black citizens were included in the plan. The appeals went unheard. White liberals were silent. Along with the placement of a new highway that cut through Brooklyn, plowing under homes and commerce, urban renewal erased Brooklyn. In the 1960s, the city tore down almost 1,500 structures and displaced more than 1,000 families.

As Charlotte went, so went cities from coast to coast. Nationwide, more than two thousand urban renewal redevelopment projects on 1,000 square miles of urban land were undertaken between 1949 and 1973, when the urban renewal program officially ended. Roughly 600,000 housing units were demolished, displacing two million people. Thousands of small businesses were forced to close.[11] Many cities have their own Brooklyn story, and every citizen ought to know it because these stories are far from over and done. They shaped our towns and cities for decades. They shape us all still.

In Charlotte, the promised "renewal" fell far short, at least for the hundreds of Black families who were displaced. In the place of the homes and businesses that once comprised Brooklyn, the city and county governments built public buildings, including City Hall, a now-abandoned public school headquarters, a courthouse, a park, and a jail. A muscular, well-fortified Federal Reserve building where currency is removed from circulation and chopped into confetti-size bits occupies one block, a symbol of Charlotte's banking prowess. Several blocks owned by real estate investors and developers still sit empty.

Then came yet another overhaul. In 2019, Mecklenburg County contracted with a Chicago developer that planned a $683-million project to build hundreds of thousands of square feet of office, retail, restaurant, and hotel space over seventeen acres of what was Brooklyn. Caldwell Presbyterian Church, where I serve as pastor, and others in the Presbytery of Charlotte joined a group of advocates that pressed the developer and the city and county governments, which were land-owning partners in the venture, to view the development as an opportunity to repair, in part, what had happened to Brooklyn. We asked for 20 percent of the apartments to be affordable, for 20 percent of the business/commercial space to be reserved for African American–owned businesses and for rental subsidies to be provided for those businesses, and for a portion of the development's income be used to create a restorative justice fund.

The developer refused and sat on the property, which increased in value from $27 million to $35 million, not counting a 1.56-acre parcel the developer later put up for sale for $8.2 million. In early 2024, the developer pledged to make 10 to 12 percent of the 1,200 housing units in the mixed-use development affordable. The developer then said the entire build could take at least another twelve years.[12]

Brooklyn's experience was repeated in the nearby Greenville neighborhood of mostly Black residents. Less than a mile away, however, the mostly white neighborhood where Caldwell Presbyterian resides faced some of the same forces of redevelopment but came away with a different outcome. By the 1960s and '70s, the once affluent Elizabeth neighborhood was showing the effects of white flight and suburbanization. Built for some of the city's leaders in commerce, many of its grand, older homes had been divided into apartments for hippies and other urban "pioneers." Its four churches, including Caldwell, were struggling as many of their members moved out and on to newer churches.

Under the same federal highway-building program that gutted Brooklyn, authorities proposed a highway cloverleaf that would have taken down many of Elizabeth's houses, then occupied almost exclusively by white folk. But even in its weakened state, Elizabeth prevailed. Neighbors created the Elizabeth Community Association and successfully deflected the full damage of the project. The highway went through, cutting the neighborhood in half, but the damage was scaled down from original proposals. Now the median home price in Elizabeth is $820,000, and homes sell regularly for $1 million to $2 million.[13]

A Surprising (to some) Wake-Up Call
Stirs the City's Power Brokers

In the decades that followed this redevelopment, Charlotte's sins sat under the surface, out of sight and out of mind, at least for the many white folks who were not touched by their lasting, tectonic legacies. Charlotte looked like a storybook success, a city that literally and figuratively emanated ever outward from the intersection of commerce and power. Its success drew newcomers by the hundreds of thousands. From 1980 to 2014, fed in part by an influx of Latino arrivals attracted by the abundance of good-paying jobs, the population more than doubled. The percentage of people of color living in the county rose from 24 to 52 percent.[14] Charlotte took its place among other major metros as a majority-minority city. Leaders prided themselves in building a sparkling city of the future. But all that was on the surface.

In 2000, Harvard public policy scholar Robert Putnam produced a nationwide Social Capital Benchmark Survey. It ranked Charlotte as one of the nation's fastest-growing cities and one of the best in which to live and work. The city also rated among the highest for its philanthropy. So far, so good, many civic boosters thought. But there were other reasons Charlotte stood out that its chamber of commerce didn't welcome. Charlotte, Putnam found, had particularly low interracial trust compared to almost every other city in the study. In a 2015 interview he concluded, "History has bequeathed Charlotte and other Southern cities a high level of inequality. That goes back centuries, frankly. There are some things Charlotte has done that are moving in the right direction, and some things where Charlotte has more work to do."[15] Thus the truth of the "two Charlottes," which residents of color had long known, became more undeniable for the city's powerful, white decision-makers. Putnam's subsequent studies of the city in 2008 and 2011 showed little progress.

In 2014, Harvard economist Raj Chetty and his fellow researchers rattled the city's feel-good vibe all over again. Their national study, titled "Where Is the Land of Opportunity?," exposed Charlotte's dirty secret that not everyone had a chance to make it if they tried. Out of fifty metro areas in the study, the city ranked last in economic mobility.[16] Of those areas, a child born into the lowest income levels in Charlotte had worse odds of moving into the top fifth of the income distribution over their lifetime than a child in any of the remaining forty-nine metro areas. Children born into only slightly better economic circumstances had only slightly better chances of climbing out of poverty. An article in *The Atlantic* put it starkly: "Data suggests that Charlotte is a dead-end for people trying to escape poverty," reporter Alana Semuels wrote.[17]

The city and the nation took note. Civic leaders organized carefully facilitated public conversations and launched numerous task forces. More studies were written, and tens of millions of dollars were raised from the corporate, philanthropic, and public sectors to fund solutions to Charlotte's economic mobility problem. The efforts were authentic and well intended. In subsequent years, follow-up studies showed some improvement, but the city remained in a catch-22 of its own making: explosive growth always outpaced the solutions to its problems.

In September 2016, the underlying tension broke through. Charlotte police shot and killed a Black man, Keith Lamont Scott, who had been sitting in his car. In an uprising, justifiably frustrated and angered residents took to the streets of Uptown Charlotte, flowing through its canyons of corporate towers and putting the city in the spotlight on national news for several nights in a row. Marching in those protests, I felt a deep resolve and a hope that something might change. Something *had* to change.

Housing and Homelessness
Exposed as Core Challenges

As much as anything, these events exposed Charlotte's underlying challenges of housing and homelessness. The city had much to think about—and to do—to repair the damage done in prior decades if it was going to address issues of poverty and social and economic immobility. City leaders and advocates for the marginalized focused on homelessness as fundamental to the city's housing challenges and turned their attention to "rapid-response" strategies to try to house those in need. Advocates, elected officials, and nonprofit partners embraced a strategy called "housing first," which is described by the National Alliance to End Homelessness:

> Housing First is a homeless assistance approach that prioritizes providing permanent housing to people experiencing homelessness, providing them some stability to focus on ways to improve their lives. This approach is guided by the belief that people need basic necessities like food and a place to live before attending to anything less critical, such as getting a job, budgeting properly, or attending to substance use issues. Additionally, Housing First is based on the understanding that client choice is valuable in housing selection and supportive service participation, and that exercising that choice is likely to make a client more successful in remaining housed and improving their life.[18]

This data-proven approach showed results. With the goal to end homelessness for veterans and the chronically homeless in Charlotte, a collaborative of service providers housed more than one thousand in a four-year period. This was a moment of hope among housing advocates, but it was short-lived.

As the COVID-19 pandemic came and went in 2019–2020, Charlotte's housing crisis worsened at every level. The pandemic intensified the city's shortage of housing of all types, and the impact fell heaviest on the most vulnerable. Charlotte followed the national trend: more people than ever moved out of homelessness but as many or more lost their housing. While several new housing strategies had helped, the causal factors didn't slow. In all this, Charlotte reflected nationwide facts. Jeff Olivet, executive director of the U.S. Interagency Council on Homelessness, said, "We've gotten very, very good at providing supportive housing for people. We've not done a great job of turning off the faucet."[19]

Charlotte's continued inflow of upwardly mobile, new residents drove construction prices and rental prices skyward. In one year, 2021, rents rose faster than in almost every other American city.[20] A person earning the minimum wage would have to work 116 hours a week to afford a one-bedroom apartment at fair market rent.[21] Beyond the rental market, the pain was felt just as much by potential homebuyers. In 2019, a $75,000-a-year salary could afford a median-priced home in Charlotte. By 2022, the salary needed to buy the same home had more than doubled to $163,750. As rental costs surged nationwide, they went even higher in Charlotte. In 2022, of twenty-nine metro areas where year-over-year rental prices increased more than the national median, Charlotte was one of four with the highest increases across bedroom types, reaching a median of $1,981 a month.[22] The data showed that Charlotte's peers in size and population, including Cleveland, Milwaukee-Waukesha, Nashville, Kansas City, and Columbus, also had fast-spreading affordability problems. The nation's housing crisis had become an every-town problem.

In response, voters approved hundreds of millions in funding for new affordable housing in the 2022 midterm elections. Charlotte voters added another $50 million to the $200 million that voters had approved in prior years. That amount was matched by corporate funders. But the need continued to outgrow the supply. With a need for at least 35,000 additional affordable housing units, Charlotte's housing crisis required an all-hands, locally driven response. A growing number of the city's churches heard the call.

A City of Churches

Charlotte prides itself as a city of churches.

Presbyterian Scots-Irish immigrants arrived in the Carolinas in the middle of the eighteenth century. Many of the city's most prominent roads in Charlotte's nicest neighborhoods were named for the churches Presbyterians planted, such as Providence, Sharon, Sardis, and Amity. Charlotte remains one of the nation's most Presbyterian-dense cities. Evangelist Billy Graham grew up on a dairy farm on the outskirts of town, where a museum and library now stand in his honor.

The city's religious history reaches well beyond the Presbyterians. As the first bishop of the United House of Prayer for All People, Charles Manuel "Sweet Daddy" Grace built a branch of the twenty-nine-state denomination in Charlotte. He was widely known in the early to mid-twentieth century for his faith healings, lively worship services, and huge parades in Charlotte's Brooklyn community. In nearby Fort Mill, South Carolina, the creators of the PTL Television Network, Jim and Tammy Faye Bakker, scammed tens of thousands of loyal viewers. As with other major metros, Charlotte diversified over time, along with its multifaith complexion.

The city's most powerful and well-resourced churches and houses of faith, white and Black, have contributed tens of millions of dollars to address social needs over the decades. With the data of Charlotte's housing and economic disparities, many of its churches heard a new call to house their neighbors.

New Partnerships, Deep Investments

In 2008, eight years after the cannon shot of Robert Putnam's social capital study, Myers Park Presbyterian Church stepped up. One of the largest churches of its denomination in the Carolinas and long a home to some of the city's most affluent and powerful families, the congregation focused on the nearby, century-old, and historically Black neighborhood known as Grier Heights. The two neighborhoods had long been associated. For decades, Grier Heights residents rode the bus to work in the prestigious homes of Myers Park as "domestic help" and groundskeepers.

The church's complicated relationship with Grier Heights prompted it to create CrossRoads, a faith-based nonprofit dedicated to working to address the city's growing inequities in a particular neighborhood. In a partnership including two Black houses of faith in Grier Heights, Antioch Baptist and Grier Heights Presbyterian, CrossRoads studied neighborhood needs and responded with a multipronged strategy for community development. In 2019, Myers Park Presbyterian followed up with a $950,000, zero-interest loan to the Charlotte-Mecklenburg Housing Partnership (later renamed DreamKey Partners) to develop affordable multifamily housing in Grier Heights.

A public-private partnership, DreamKey is the city's longtime leader in building affordable housing for a range of populations. It partnered also with Covenant Presbyterian Church for a $2-million investment to build apartments for those earning 30, 50, 60, and 80 percent of the area median income. Covenant followed in 2021 with an additional $400,000 gift to the local Habitat for Humanity chapter for purchasing nine acres of land from Greater Bethel AME Church, where thirty-four new affordable homes would be built.

In 2021, Myers Park United Methodist Church made two major gifts to ease the housing crisis. It pledged $1 million to Habitat to create thirty-nine affordable, for-sale homes in a partnership with Habitat for Humanity. Its second $1-million grant became a cornerstone of Caldwell Presbyterian's funding to build supportive housing on its campus. This gift to Caldwell was in honor of a much-loved member, Richard Harrison, whom the two congregations shared, who lived in permanent supportive housing.

Across town, one of the city's largest and most prominent Black churches, the Park Church, broke ground in 2021 on an eighty-unit senior-living apartment complex for those earning 30 percent of the area median income. Through its community development corporation (CDC), the Park Church launched a master-planning process for a mixed-use development on a separate twenty-three-acre parcel of land.

Each of these initiatives advanced what Charlotte's churches were willing to do to house their neighbors. Many of those neighbors were, in fact, descended from or had other close connections to the families affected by the city's legacies of displacement and separation. Directly and indirectly, church-led housing projects, both Black and white, addressed the city's lasting sins.

Echoes and Answers to Brooklyn's Destruction

When the bulldozers of urban renewal leveled Brooklyn and displaced more than a thousand families, twelve churches were either destroyed or relocated. Their member families scattered, and the latter generations are still among those struggling in an increasingly affluent and exclusive city. One by one, the close-in neighborhoods where they relocated are being gentrified. Landlords are increasing rents, and property taxes are going up on homeowners with limited incomes.

Several of the city's Black churches, all connected to Brooklyn in one way or another, have offered an answer. Charlotte's earliest example of a church-based housing initiative is Grace Emmanuel Baptist's Emmanuel Homes. Located just beyond the boundaries of what was once Brooklyn, Grace led the way in the 1980s, building fifty apartments in part for those who had been displaced years earlier.

St. Paul Baptist Church also has direct ties to Brooklyn's erasure. In the final days of 2004, Rev. Greg Moss had begun to plan the church's annual Watch Night observance—a New Year's Eve tradition in the Black church that commemorates the night enslaved and free Black Americans celebrated the new year on January 1, 1863, when the Emancipation Proclamation took effect. As Moss looked out over his city, he saw too many of his neighbors contending with a different kind of captivity. He saw those being displaced by rising housing and rental costs. He saw others on the streets with no place to live and not enough support. Moss decided to announce that, after the worship service, members would be invited to spend the night outside to better understand the lives of those with no housing at all.

About thirty members accepted Moss's invitation. They retired to a camp of cardboard boxes arrayed outside the church buildings. A chilling rain fell on the overnighters, who took turns going into the sanctuary to pray and get warm for a moment. In the wee hours after midnight, other church members and friends dropped off hot coffee and warm scarves on their way home from their New Year's celebrations.

When the sun rose for the first time in 2005, a new dawn broke for the members of St. Paul. With that memorable Watch Night in mind, church members began to explore how it might offer its neighbors freedom from the ruthless forces of the deepening housing crisis in the nation's second-largest banking center. "That night gave us a jump start to expanding people's vision to the need and what was possible," Moss recalls. "We just kept going after that."

The decision summoned other memories for many St. Paul members. They recalled when the city forced the congregation out of Brooklyn by urban renewal (or "urban removal" as Moss calls it). After being run out of Brooklyn in the 1960s, St. Paul's members wanted to control their own fate. From the 1970s through the 1990s, property values in Charlotte's Belmont area, anchored in what had been one of Charlotte's mill neighborhoods, remained depressed. Over time, the church acquired several blocks of land adjacent to the church, which it used for parking.

Even the security of additional property was not enough for some. Some church members raised the possibility of moving the church again, this time to the suburbs, Moss recalled. "There was a time when St. Paul had basically become a drive-in church of members who lived in further-out neighborhoods," Moss says. "But we made a commitment to stay, and it gave the church a chance to more deeply connect with the community." After the Watch Night out in the cold rain, the church prayed—and turned its mission focus to housing, ready to offer what it had. "St. Paul was land rich and cash poor," Moss recalls.

Church leaders formed a CDC and assembled a team of people with knowledge of real estate, law, finance, and other needed skills. As one of the city's earliest movers in housing, St. Paul was one of the first recipients of funds from the city's rotating, voter-funded Housing Trust Fund. Other construction funding came from investors who received a tax credit for investing in low-income housing, as well as a direct investment from Bank of America. It leased the church's land, creating an ongoing revenue stream for the church.

The church partnered with Laurel Street Residential, a mixed-income housing developer and a Charlotte pioneer in working with churches to build housing. Together they developed a vision of a village for people from different circumstances, and this village opened in 2017: sixty units of senior housing, twenty-three units of apartments, and twenty-nine townhomes, all targeted to those earning 60 percent of the area median income.

"Anything Is Possible"

Another church with connections to Brooklyn is Little Rock AME Zion Church, one of the city's most prominent and oldest Black congregations. The national publishing house of the African Methodist Episcopal Zion denomination had been a major part of life in Brooklyn, and many of the congregation's members had roots in what had been Brooklyn. With that heritage in mind, members relocated the entire church there years after Brooklyn's destruction.

The church was thriving when it called Rev. Dr. Dwayne Walker as its pastor in 2006. It occupied a prominent uptown corner a few blocks from the direct center of the city's skyscrapers. Behind it was a mix of a few surviving mill houses surrounded by the kind of newer, high-end residential construction that was spreading like kudzu across uptown. The blocks to its west were filled with townhomes that served as public and lower-rent homes, where many of those displaced when Brooklyn was mowed down came to live.

By 2018, the center-city housing boom had literally reached Little Rock's front door. With it came serious considerations for the congregation. With the memory of Brooklyn's demise in mind, the church moved to control its own fate, just as St. Paul's had. "I saw the community was changing and I wanted to make sure Little Rock was not going to be sitting here and watching all this happen *to* us," Walker recalls. The church had purchased an adjacent piece of property. It also launched a CDC grounded in Peter's response to the beggar in Acts 3:6: "I have no silver or gold, but what I have I give you; in the name of Jesus Christ of Nazareth, stand up and walk."

When it began to envision housing, the CDC's first proposal was to provide seventy new apartment units on the land it had to offer. City officials encouraged the church to strive for more impact and offered to donate land it owned adjacent to the church. The result was a community of 105 apartments, half affordable and half market rate. Working with Laurel Street Residential as a partner, the church funded the $15-million development through the city's Housing Trust Fund, investor tax credits, and bond and bank financing.

The development was named "Varick on 7th" to honor the first bishop of the AME Zion Church. Little Rock owns 67 percent of the project, which opened its doors in 2024. Developer Laurel Street owns 33 percent, and the church retains ownership of the land. Laurel Street manages the property. The church's CDC will create programming based on the residents' needs, such as workforce training, youth mentoring, a food pantry, or a clothing closet.

As Walker looks out from the church and sees the new apartments in the foreground of the city's shining skyline, he smiles broadly. Through faith, Little Rock found a way, even years later, to respond to the displacement from Brooklyn's destruction, creating an affordable place in the heart of the city for seniors and others with limited incomes.

"Anything is possible," says the distinguished, smartly dressed preacher who is not shy to take a stand on other social justice issues. "We serve a big God. The Bible says, 'You have not because you ask not.' We've put the needs together with the resources. It's like the old candy bar commercial where the chocolate and the peanut butter get together to make something new. . . . We all brought our resources to bear."

To continue to tackle the city's challenges requires ongoing collaboration, Walker says: "We can't continue to work in silos. We have to work together. When need meets opportunity, the possibilities are endless."

Creating a Place of Healing in a Trauma-Torn Community

A few miles to the northeast of its center city, Charlotte's Hidden Valley neighborhood is a community divided, whipsawed over decades by waves of change and threat. The faithful of Mayfield Memorial Baptist Church offer what they hope will be a place of healing, reconciliation, and community.

Built in the early 1960s, Hidden Valley offered modest, neatly kept ranch homes with spacious yards and winding streets named after storybook themes and characters: Cinderella Road, Candy Stick Lane, and Snow White Street. It began as a mostly white, working-class neighborhood. But when the city tore down the Brooklyn neighborhood, many of those who were displaced resettled in Hidden Valley. With racial integration, tensions spiked. Hidden Valley saw a few instances of home shootings and cross burnings. But residents rallied to calm the neighborhood and advocated to protect the community.

Then came legally forced busing in the 1970s. Many neighborhood kids were bused to schools across town. Other, mostly white kids were bused in to attend the neighborhood elementary school. Busing advanced school integration on the whole. But busing neighborhood kids away undercut residents' sense of connection to the neighborhood school.

Still, neighbors rallied and remained loyal—only to see more change. In the 1980s, Charlotte's growth necessitated the widening of the neighborhood's major thoroughfare from two lanes to four, bringing more traffic and heavier commercial development.

Yet Hidden Valley's hardest decade was still to come. In the 1990s, a violent gang, the Hidden Valley Kings, launched a robust, citywide drug trade. With the Kings came unwanted local and national notoriety and media coverage. Some neighbors fled, and real estate values dropped. Again, however, the neighborhood rallied and stood its ground.

By 2007, the neighborhood's most prominent church, Mayfield Memorial Baptist, called Rev. Dr. Peter Wherry as pastor. He brought a prophetic, justice-oriented theology that challenged the congregation to look outward into its neighborhood. Under his leadership, the church acquired several homes on lots adjacent to the church. Some were crack houses, others flophouses.

By 2008, the key leaders of the Hidden Valley Kings had been arrested and imprisoned. Crime dropped over the next several years, and neighborhood property values began to recover. The "Valley" was also diversifying, gaining more of the Latino residents moving to Charlotte for its humming economy. Tensions rose as longtime homeowners adjusted to the Latino influx.

Then within the same few years, Hidden Valley experienced the strange paradox that was hitting many of the city's close-in neighborhoods: A growing number of unhoused people arrived in the neighborhood, spending their days in the streets and camping in the neighborhood's wooded areas. At the same time, Charlotte's economic vitality and growth had attracted investors seeking to buy up depressed properties. They swooped into Hidden Valley and began acquiring single-family homes at low prices, some flipping the properties for a quick buck.

Then came corporate landlords, large investment groups that acquire single-family homes and rent out one bedroom at a time for up to $1,000 and $2,000 a month.[23] The corporate landlord trend hit Hidden Valley hard, accounting for up to one in five home purchases at its peak in 2022. Longtime residents in Hidden Valley expressed concern that the influx of renters destabilized the community, replacing longtime homeowners with more transient residents less invested in the neighborhood.[24]

As its neighborhood experienced continued waves of change, so did the Mayfield Memorial congregation. It was shifting from being a "traditional," inward-facing church to one that embraced a more justice-rooted, outward-facing mission. Charlotte's uprisings, racial reckoning, and economic injustices galvanized the congregation's sense of mission. The congregation turned its attention to the church-adjacent properties it had collected over the past three decades and began to dream.

When Mayfield first proposed constructing a mixed-income village of homes on the land it had amassed, it didn't go over well. After decades of change and challenges, longtime area homeowners greeted the idea of more affordable housing with caution and lots of questions. Wherry explains, "Due to persistent misunderstandings in the community as to whether the 'village' concept would bring congestion and crime, the church and its CDC opted to avoid acrimonious court battles by reverting to our long-standing 'Plan B.'"

Plan B was a single building of fifty-one apartments with additional spaces for community services and mental health care. Named Sugaree Place to honor the Indigenous people who first settled the area, it offered one-bedroom units for about $400 a month to those at 30 percent of the area median income and three-bedroom units for as low as $547 a month. The $14.4-million cost was covered through a combination of funds from the city's Housing Trust Fund, investor tax credits, a mortgage, a grant from Covenant Presbyterian Church, and financing from Mayfield's developer, Dream-Key Partners.

On a spring afternoon as subcontractors scurried to put the final touches on a handsome new building that held the dreams of so many, I invited the stakeholders of the venture to share their experience in the venture. We gathered in an unfinished ground-floor space that would house community-oriented services. Nearby homes reflected the diversity and complexity of contemporary Hidden Valley. In one yard, two young Latino girls played in a plastic swimming pool while a chicken pecked in the grass. Elsewhere, neatly trimmed lawns sat alongside homes where multiple cars spilled out of the driveway into the yard.

Next to Wherry sat longtime Mayfield trustee Delores Reid-Smith. A tireless church and community leader, she stood by the church through its decades of challenge and change, time and again demonstrating resilience born of her faith. (Said Wherry, "If you see Delores and a bear getting into an argument, you'd better worry about the bear.") "I've watched how the neighborhood has changed," she said. "And Pastor Wherry's leadership heightened our awareness of what's happening in the neighborhood." An after-school program will occupy space in Sugaree Place to work with the residents and neighborhood children and their families.

Sugaree Place will also serve more broadly as a hub of community and healing. David Roundtree, a therapist and clinical social worker, has worked with former members of the Hidden Valley Kings and developed bonds with them, their families, and their neighbors. He plans space in Sugaree Place to offer trauma-informed care to the change-battered and hurting neighborhood. Roundtree gives the church and its leadership credit for staying put, taking risk, and reaching out even in the face of opposition. "There is always some animus that comes when you do the work of God," he says, reflecting on the sometimes bumpy path the church traveled to realize its dream. "I am sure the church has some needed repairs on its own buildings, but I see them building housing for others. That speaks volumes. It's why I am here."

Sugaree Place and the church's multipronged, neighborhood-focused CDC represent a lasting stand against all the forces—social, cultural, and economic—that have besieged the neighborhood over decades. "What we are doing here is speaking out against structural evil—systemic issues that had to be addressed in concrete ways," Wherry says. "This will outlive all of us. My vision is that every one of every class and culture can be seen as deserving a good shot in life."

"We Need to Think Generations Ahead": The Power of a Land Trust

Other faith organizations work on a smaller but equally important grassroots basis. In 2005, shortly after graduating from seminary, Baptist pastors Greg and Helms Jarrell moved into the Enderly Park neighborhood in mostly Black and lower-income West Charlotte. The couple envisioned a ministry patterned after a Catholic Worker house, living in solidarity, demonstrating hospitality to all, meeting the neighbors where they were. As Charlotte calls itself the "Queen City," their vision became known as "QC Family Tree."

Like so many neighborhoods, Enderly Park has been through waves of changes. The land had been a farm owned by Confederate veteran S. B. Alexander, a devout member of First Presbyterian Church, one of the city's oldest congregations. After his death, his children parceled out the land for single-family homes beginning in the 1920s. The neighborhood gradually filled out until the 1950s.

What began as a segregated white neighborhood (the first deeds included racial restrictions on landownership) shifted to Black ownership by the 1970s. Once again, Charlotte's legacies came to bear as Black families who lost housing in Brooklyn's destruction displaced some families to Enderly Park. With their arrival, some white neighbors took flight. As suburban sprawl redirected public resources and infrastructure improvements to the new white neighborhoods to the southeast, Enderly Park suffered sustained disinvestment through the end of the twentieth century.

QC Family Tree's mission was to live amid and work alongside the families of the neglected neighborhood. With whatever financial

backing they could find, QC Family Tree began by assembling properties one at a time to offer stabilized, affordable rent. Meanwhile,
the Jarrells and the supporters of their ministry responded to their
neighbors' needs. They ministered to the youth and met neighbors
where they were in life with ideas, love, the gospel, and connections
to resources. The Jarrells earned the trust of the neighbors and rode
with them through every storm.

QC Family Tree acquired four homes to house their neighbors
at affordable rates. Over time, however, Charlotte's prosperity
drove up the costs of living and housing until inflated housing prices
reached Enderly Park. Investors quietly began buying and flipping
houses. Gentrifiers began replacing the modest, brick homes with
much larger, new structures that occupied almost every inch of the
neighborhood's small lots and loomed over the remaining neighbors.
The Jarrells saw the writing on the wall. "QC had been working on
a small-scale, relational basis," Greg says. "We realized we were not
going to be able to make a dent. We needed millions of dollars to
keep up, and that was not going to happen."

For months, the leaders of QC Family Tree met with a group of
west-side stakeholders, Black pastors, business owners, advocates,
and other leaders. What emerged was a new idea—a land trust to
acquire and hold property to stem the tide of displacement and
property speculation. The newly formed West Side Community
Land Trust was the first of its kind in Charlotte. Its model of invit-
ing "patient capital" attracted supporters and investors, allowing
the trust to acquire property and combat the quick-hit, in-and-out
wave of property flippers. One retired doctor, for example, invested
about $650,000 of funds he would not need until later in his life. His
and others' support enabled the land trust to acquire several houses
and several dozen acres of vacant land across Charlotte's west side,
Greg says.

The land trust attracted tens of millions of dollars in investment.
Organizers hired a small staff, soon scoring victories in building new
affordable properties and preserving existing housing. Its first development was an apartment building composed of 120 affordable units
for seniors. Next, it partnered with Mecklenburg County government
to purchase thirty-two homes in Charlotte's Hoskins neighborhood

northwest of Uptown. The county's $6-million infusion will allow the land trust to renovate the homes, offering some for rent and others for sale. The acquisition in August 2023 brought the total number of homes in the land trust's portfolio to 162.

"We needed a fifty-year solution to stop the real estate speculation," Greg says of the land trust strategy. "We need to change our imaginations. We need to think generations ahead if we are ever going to solve our problems."

A Different Kind of Legacy in the Heart of the City

Back on Tryon Street in the direct heart of Charlotte, the people of First United Methodist Church tell their own stories about generations of faithful thinking and acting to serve the city's unhoused as the hands and feet of Christ. Its journey began in the early 2000s with what started out as a simple "muffin ministry" to provide breakfast to those on the streets on Sunday mornings. Now, as with other urban churches, the congregation plans a campus makeover that is its newest commitment to loving neighbor and helping solve Charlotte's housing crisis.

First Methodist's stately, gothic, stone sanctuary holds its own alongside Uptown's glass-and-marble bank headquarters and other office towers and high-rise, high-rent apartment buildings. Its campus speaks of how the city's power and faith have always intersected. One of the most beautiful in the city, its sanctuary was funded in part by James B. Duke, who built the region's electric utility that grew to meet the textile industry's demand for power. When it was completed in 1927, the sanctuary could hold 1,200 people. It represented Methodists' highest hopes—and those hopes came true for a while. The congregation numbered 5,000 people at its height in the mid-twentieth century, including many of the city's most powerful families and power brokers. Its buildings hummed with activities on Sundays and through the week.

As in so many other cases, however, white flight and suburbanization in the 1960s and 1970s drained the center-city church of thousands of its members. A core group remained, but their commitment would be further tested. When its pastors preached support for the civil rights movement in the 1960s, the KKK called in bomb threats. Later the church extended a generous welcome and authentic embrace of the city's growing LGBTQ community.

But it was another calling that really redefined the congregation. Charlotte's numbers of unhoused neighbors began to grow significantly in the 1990s. The leadership of several center-city churches huddled with business leaders and launched a nonprofit agency dedicated to helping those on the streets stabilize their lives. The initial muffin ministry grew from serving dozens to hundreds before church every Sunday. Members and staff developed relationships with some of the neighbors, who helped set up for the meal and interceded when guests had disagreements. During the week, the church didn't try to run off its unhoused neighbors. It dug deeper to understand their struggles. It launched a clothing closet and later an arts program that invited unhoused neighbors to tell their stories.

When members learned one man on the streets, a diabetic, was hiding his insulin in a nearby creek to keep it cool, they shared a door code with him so that he could keep his medicine in a basement refrigerator. Members found other ways to help their church neighbors, building trust and partnership even more deeply. It wasn't easy, but members rose to the challenge, and serving the unhoused moved from the periphery of the church's life to become one of its defining ministries.

In 2020, First Methodist began its "Second Century" discernment process. It yielded a new dream to expand its role in addressing the city's housing crisis. The church entered a partnership with a Charlotte developer, gruppoETICO, to create a multistory building offering mixed-income housing, pairing market-rate apartments with those at several tiers of affordable rent. The church will put in two-thirds of an acre of land and agree to tear down two large, partially used buildings to make way for the new structure. As codeveloper, the church will receive a portion of the venture's income, a steady and welcome supplement to its members' tithes and offerings.

The church also earns rental income through partnership with a range of arts and choral groups that perform concerts in the picturesque, soaring sanctuary. With that ministry in mind, the dream includes building a new "front door" atrium structure on what is now an open plaza leading to Tryon Street. It will connect the sanctuary with the street and create a gathering place where campus residents can blend with lovers of the arts and all can enjoy concerts and shows together. For the members of the congregation, it is a natural extension of who they have come to be—a mix of LGBTQ folks working alongside young families and longtime members to care for those who are often ignored and avoided in the city's bustling business district.

Serving their most immediate, unhoused neighbors has been "a challenge but a good challenge," says Rev. Dr. Val Rosenquist, who came to First Methodist in 2015. "There are sacrifices that sometimes have to be made, and we sometimes get exhausted," she says. "But it has brought us together as a congregation. We really understand that we're working together. If one member says they are going to show up to help with something, another member will say, 'I'm not going to let you show up by yourself.' There is a lot of dedication to one another in addition to serving our neighbors."

"When there is a need, people come out of the woodwork, and that is really wonderful. They know they are making a difference. . . . It's what we mean when we say, 'We practice inclusion and pursue justice.' Those are our values around here."

Giving Easter a Place to Live

In the same years that First Methodist paused to consider the possibilities for its future, so did Caldwell Presbyterian. In 2013, after celebrating their church's centennial, Caldwell folk turned to God to ask for direction in what they boldly claimed would be the congregation's "second century." With the church's reboot well underway since its near closing in 2006, members dreamed big and small. Over several months we met in town halls and listening sessions. The conversations generated a list of sixty-eight ideas. (The eyes of Caldwell's parishioners are often bigger than their stomachs.) The proposals ranged from the small to the audacious. But one stood out. Shaped by its three years of hosting a fifty-bed homeless shelter, Caldwell decided to go big on housing.

The church spent the next year studying local housing issues and assessing the range of needs across the housing spectrum. With a new context and perspective on the crisis, the congregation chose to take on a challenging vision: providing "housing first," permanent supportive housing to those earning no more than 50 percent of the area median income. It set aside its fourteen-thousand-square-foot former Christian education building, which had been a laboratory and incubator for a range of experiments in ministry, for a fifty-year commitment as housing. Its old classrooms, where Presbyterians had studied Scripture and youth had memorized catechisms, would become a place of living lessons.

The building had the space for twenty-one studio apartments for those who had been chronically homeless—that is, those who had recently spent at least a year on the streets or been repeatedly homeless while struggling with a disabling condition such as a serious mental illness, substance use disorder, or physical disability. The church turned to Charlotte's DreamKey as development partner. DreamKey brought vital contacts to funders and public funding sources though little experience in working with churches. We would learn together.

The pandemic and Charlotte's superheated construction market drove construction prices upward, but the partners finally raised the $6 million the building conversion required (see appendix C). Funding consisted of a range of partners from the public, private, and philanthropic sectors, along with the church's own donation of the building, land, and $800,000 from a capital campaign. Myers Park United Methodist, with whom Caldwell shared a beloved member and leader who lived in supportive housing, generously extended $1 million from its own capital campaign. Combined, the funding allowed the church to pay for the project without long-term debt, enabling effective rents for the apartments to be among the lowest in the city. A big part of Caldwell's learning curve has been clarity about the limits of our qualifications and expertise. So to manage the operations and provide the supportive services needed, the church entered a partnership with Roof Above, the city's primary agency serving the unhoused and others in need of deeply affordable housing.

When it came time to name the initiative, the congregation looked back to a poignant and painful part of its history—the fortune left to the church in 1922 that came from the Caldwell family's prosperous, antebellum plantation in northern Mecklenburg County. It was a story that was new to all of us. Because most of the Caldwell congregation came after the church almost closed in 2006, none of us had slowed down to trace the full history of the church. As we celebrated the church's centennial in 2012, a wise and dutiful elder, Beth Van Gorp, took it upon herself to read one hundred years of session minutes. When she uncovered the truth about how the church had changed its name from John Knox to Caldwell after receiving its wealth, the facts fell hard on all members, particularly those of color.

The church needed time to digest the news that the funds that built our beloved sanctuary, where we gathered as one on Sundays, were wrought from the labor and agony of those the Caldwell family enslaved. Suddenly, Sundays together felt different, and we have done a lot of talking ever since.

In many ways, we are still grappling with the legacy. That truth informs our ongoing journey as an intersectional community of faith that is learning and practicing the ways of antiracism, not just acknowledging the sin of racism but striving to learn how to deconstruct it inside and outside the life of the church. Every Sunday as worship begins, we acknowledge the source of the Caldwell fortune, also noting that the land where the church sits was taken from its original occupants, those of the Catawba, Waxhaw, and Sugaree nations.

Informed by this past, the elders chose to call the new community "Easter's Home," to honor a woman named "Easter" whom the Caldwell family had enslaved. The name lifted up a woman who did not have true freedom but whose toil, along with that of so many others, should be remembered. Her name reminds us to strive to be people of the resurrection every day.

Habitat for Humanity: How One Leader Has Worked to Keep Up in a City of Affluence

Since opening its office in 1983, Habitat for Humanity of the Charlotte Region has partnered with dozens of faith communities of all kinds. Habitat brings a much-needed link in the chain of affordable housing options—for-sale, single-family homes, earned through dozens of hours of sweat equity invested by its low-income buyers who work alongside volunteers to build and repair homes. By acquiring open land in often overlooked working-class and lower-income areas of town, Habitat Charlotte Region has produced 1,500 homes within financial reach of low- and middle-income families, allowing the owners to build equity and end the cycle of displacement.

But as Charlotte's economy roared on into the 2000s and beyond, even proven models like Habitat's struggled to keep up with land costs and building expenses. For example, a Habitat home sold to a family in 1989 for $38,500 later found itself amid a wave of gentrification. The home was sold and razed. In its place now stands a home that sold in 2022 for $1.3 million.[25] Gentrification knows no bounds.

Another example of a congregation making all the difference is Greater Bethel AME Church. Years earlier, the Black congregation had purchased a wooded nine-acre tract with a home, thinking it might be a suitable parsonage for the pastor. But the land was across town from the church. Adjacent to established neighborhoods and with major thoroughfare connections to Uptown, the land grew in value. As church leaders considered their options, eager developers met with them, offering high market prices that would have supported the construction of homes selling for $400,000 and more.

But theirs were not the voices that the Rev. Dr. Abdue Knox heard one day as he walked the land, seeking discernment and guidance. God spoke, as God will. Rather than cashing in at top dollar, the church opted to sell it to Habitat for $450,000. (Covenant Presbyterian funded $400,000 of the purchase.) The deal afforded Habitat land at a price far below that of much of what was available elsewhere in the city, and it will become a neighborhood of up to twenty-nine affordable homes. As part of the sale, Habitat will transfer one of the homes to Greater Bethel for it to help church members in need of housing assistance.[26]

Measuring the City's Need

As Charlotte emerged from the COVID-19 pandemic, dozens of community leaders closest to its housing crisis were wrapping up a comprehensive examination of the problems and potential solutions.

A far-reaching group of corporate executives, public officials, government leaders, housing and real estate experts, and nonprofit leaders—250 people in all—had been organized for the task. With the assistance of a team of consultants, they took months to calculate the depth of the city's housing and homelessness crisis and the potential costs to fix it, involving not just bricks-and-mortar answers but social and human services and the financial challenges of those at risk of losing their homes.[27] Among the findings were these:

- The city's many agencies and organizations focused on housing and housing-related issues needed to work together more efficiently or consider a more integrated, streamlined approach.
- Those at risk of losing their housing needed more access to affordable legal advocacy.
- About 550 individuals experiencing chronic homelessness, often struggling with mental illness, disability, or substance abuse, used services disproportionately and could be served more effectively with more intensive, individually focused care and housing support.

The United Way of Greater Charlotte was tasked with condensing and organizing the analysis into a framework for a plan. The report proposed the city could strive to become "a community where homelessness is rare, brief and non-recurring and every person has access to permanent, affordable housing and the resources to sustain it."[28] The proposed framework would focus on three areas.

First, the group proposed deeper, "person-directed care" that would address the existing "fractured and inefficient approach" to care for those on the streets or at risk of being unhoused. It envisioned a new team of "systems navigators" to work with individual cases across existing agencies and providers; development of an overarching data management system to connect an individual's needs with resources and track that person's progress; and the creation of "flexible spending accounts" to help clients access "a bundle of services," to include transportation, physical health, mental health, rental assistance, basic needs, and housing stability counseling.[29]

Second, the plan calls for the preservation of existing affordable housing. This is about doing more to interrupt the waves of displacement and gentrification. The plan would also more sharply pinpoint and act on the challenges in people's lives that most often lead to homelessness—namely, a loss of employment, a hospitalization, or family disruption.

Third, the team proposed a dramatic increase in the type, range, and volume of affordable housing. The plan would protect existing affordable housing from becoming too expensive, preserve more single-family housing, and engage landlords and apartment managers to become a bigger part of the solution. It would also significantly increase the city's existing voter-funded, rotating Housing Trust Fund to create more affordable units and provide more "permanent supportive housing" designed to address the most acute needs of the chronically unhoused (as Easter's Home does).

The United Way rolled out the ambitious framework in the summer of 2023 to a somewhat distracted city. However, in early 2024, Charlotte Mayor Vi Lyles launched an initiative to engage, educate, and equip faith-based communities interested in helping with the housing crisis.

It will be years, perhaps a generation, before we know whether it is the right prescription—and whether the city will unite behind it and invest the *billions* of dollars it will require.

A Good Start, a Mustard Seed, the Widow's Mite? All of the Above!

There are still other emerging stories of churches looking at building housing in Charlotte. In a city in need of tens of thousands of additional affordable places to live, the church projects I recount in this chapter add up to only a few hundred. Some might say that is only a drop in a bucket of need that is only getting deeper and deeper. Some elected and business leaders in Charlotte prefer more "scalable" solutions—to build as many units as fast as possible, wherever and however possible, and as cheaply as possible so that taxpayers don't raise too much of a howl. The complexity involved in building housing on church properties just isn't efficient enough, they say. It's true that God's economy—and its attention to ideas like belonging, place, and meaning—aren't what some elected officials and business-people call efficient. But these ideas have a different bottom line.

The Synoptic Gospels all include parables in which Jesus points to unlikely sources of growth and abundance. A tiny seed grows into a great tree that, in turn, becomes a home and a safe haven for a flock of birds. A small amount of yeast creates a loaf that feeds many. Maybe the fast-spreading movement of churches putting housing on their property reflects that kind of economics. Or perhaps the church-housing movement ties back to the story of the widow who quietly gives her last coin to God in gratitude for the "enough" she has. The power of the widow's mite was its example. She gave what she had, willingly and readily, without stopping to consider her own needs or consult her financial adviser.

The Charlotte churches that are building housing didn't wait for perfect answers to their abundance of questions about how to realize their dreams, God's dreams. They knowingly leaped in faith into their unendingly complex ventures. Still, the momentum of this movement in Charlotte continues to build, and more church-based developments are in the works as this book goes to press. No church has all the answers or assurances. And churches won't provide any-where near the volume of units the city needs. But their offering counts mightily in a city with plenty of legacies, both good and bad, and plenty of need.

Changing Our Imagination . . . and Acting with Urgency

Solving the housing crisis needs each city's heart and soul. It requires a change of mindset, a new way of thinking, and an alternative view of economics. Apart from spreadsheets and strategies, housing our neighbors demands a deepened commitment to interdependence, as called for so many years ago by King and others.

The choice, says longtime community advocate Kathryn Firmin Sellers, is up to the city:

> Our housing crisis is rooted in a failure to value each person's individual life. We continue to demonize and criminalize

poverty. We continue to have a system that assumes that people who are impoverished are there because they made personal mistakes along the way, instead of looking at the broader structural issues and our values as a community.

For me, housing is a fundamental human right. Unless you know where you are going to sleep at night, you simply cannot do all the things that we think people must be able to do to be successful and live with stability. . . . We have to stop thinking that the only version of the American dream is a house with a white picket fence.

We need to think about new types of housing and why it's needed. . . . We are going to need deep investment, and there's no cheap way out of this. We need to think expansively about housing. And that includes churches, particularly those with land that are proximate to economic centers and transit centers. . . . Churches' land is a very valuable asset. So I hope they feel mission-called.

For decades, Rev. Greg Jarrell and his wife, artist-activist-educator-minister Rev. Helms Jarrell, along with their boys, have lived in solidarity with the low-income, vulnerable neighbors of Enderly Park. They have fought against real estate speculators and developers seeking a quick profit. They have seen gentrifiers, even the well-intended, displace their neighbors (some of whose families were chased out of Brooklyn) and send them to seek affordable places to live in surrounding counties. They have watched as city planners proposed higher density–zoning approaches to combat spiking housing and real estate prices, only to be opposed by neighbors who think even an apartment quadruplex amid single family homes will lower their home values. It's all short-term thinking.

"We need fifty- and sixty-year solutions," Greg says. "We do need immediate solutions to stop the bleeding, yes. But to create a thriving city or even neighborhood we have to create more stability and at least slow down, if not stop, all the speculation. The way we got here was from the destruction of Brooklyn and the intrusion of new highways that divided it. From that you get white flight to the suburbs and disinvestment in poorer neighborhoods. . . . We have to create a solution that can stop the long decline of some neighborhoods only to be followed by the tidal wave of displacement. We can at least change our imaginations about what's possible."

As for generational progress, Charlotte leaders held their breath in 2024 when Harvard's research team revisited the city's progress in addressing the needs of its most disadvantaged residents. Ten years earlier, the city finished last among fifty major U.S. metros in economic mobility (a measure of what's needed to escape deep poverty). Embarrassed leaders had invested more than $200 million that improved the city's rank to a somewhat dubious 38th. It was the third-most rapid progress among cities in the study—but with far more to do. Harvard pointed to housing as one of the most important investments the city could make.

On a warm, late-spring weekday I drove over to Enderly Park to talk with Greg Jarrell, whose firsthand perspective on Charlotte's housing problems and potential is always a valued source for my learning. We sat at the dining room table in the modest craftsman bungalow where he and his wife have raised their children in solidarity with their low-income Black and Brown neighbors.

Out the front window, he sees a neighborhood that represents its city. Once called the City of Churches, it has become a busy, business-minded place conflicted between pride and dread that attracts a hundred new people every day. What he sees is a city that is only extending its long legacies of separation and displacement that hits Black and Brown people the hardest, just as always.

As we talk over my research into the church-campus housing movement, Greg seems encouraged. He knows very well that many congregations, thriving or not, have land, buildings, and social capital. Putting it to use to house our neighbors is, he says, a matter of repentance and repair: "We can trace very specifically the ways that white Christians in particular have acted against the best testimonies of our faith. So part of the work of repentance is to say, 'Hey, we got this wrong.' Our institutions did it. But we as an institution can begin helping to address the housing crisis more deeply. We can be a part of the solution rather than continuing to be a part of the problem."

He adds, "We bear that responsibility to say, 'Hey, we have to create something different. Because what we have now is two Charlottes.'"

Chapter Five

The Faces and Places of the Movement

Churches Housing Neighbors

They are, among others, Baptist, Roman Catholic, African Methodist Episcopal Zion, Episcopalian, Presbyterian, United Methodist, Lutheran, and a few Jewish congregations as well. They serve big cities and suburbs, middle-sized metros and quaint college towns. Some are thriving congregations looking with hope to the future. Others are taking a clear-eyed view of the financial bottom line and asking serious questions about the years ahead. They all face the same shifts that are reshaping the American religious landscape, particularly in Christianity. Changing demographics, declining worship attendance and member participation, and the crushing costs of maintaining buildings and grounds all constitute the kind of radical remake of the faith that takes place every five hundred years as theorized by Phyllis Tickle in her 2012 book *The Great Emergence: How Christianity Is Changing and Why.*[1] The COVID-19 pandemic accelerated the trends underneath her analysis. Add to that churches' reckoning with what hybrid congregational life—not just worship but all activities and gatherings—will need in terms of space and design.

They are ordinary people doing extraordinary things, emboldened to think out of the box and sometimes put everything on the line—as in demolishing an entire city block of church-campus buildings and moving lock, stock, and barrel to temporary quarters while the "new thing" is built, trusting there is a future there when they get back. They are the regular faithful in different settings and ministry contexts but with a shared view of the gospel's call to provide shelter in the most real sense. They serve a range of folk affected by America's housing crisis: working families, veterans and senior citizens, victims of gentrification and displacement, people with disabilities, those fighting addiction, and those living with a mix of mental health diagnoses.

As communities of faith, they must navigate the narrows of what it takes to achieve congregational consensus. They persevere through the fits and starts of fundraising, construction delays, and complications. They sift through arcane local public policy decisions and zoning codes. They assemble teams that must take on everything they don't teach you in Sunday school or seminary: intricacies of real estate development, law and finance, architecture and neighborhood engagement, social work, and processes for setting up nonprofit organizations and boards of directors.

They have new understandings of how "God's time" really works, reaching again and again for patience. Through it all, they pray and find encouragement from the word of the Lord. For each church, there is a guiding Scripture text or prayer or several. At First Presbyterian in San Mateo, California, it is to follow God's words to Isaiah about true worship and service to God and neighbor:

> "Is not this the kind of fasting I have chosen:
> to loose the chains of injustice
>   and untie the cords of the yoke,
> to set the oppressed free
>   and break every yoke?
> Is it not to share your food with the hungry
>   and to provide the poor wanderer with shelter—
> when you see the naked, to clothe them,
>   and not to turn away from your own flesh and blood?
> Then your light will break forth like the dawn,
>   and your healing will quickly appear;
> then your righteousness will go before you,
>   and the glory of the LORD will be your rear guard.

Then you will call, and the LORD will answer;
you will cry for help, and he will say: Here am I.

Isa. 58:6–9 NIV

This chapter presents the stories of a range of churches that are making way for affordable housing on their properties. We look at the state of these churches, their neighborhood contexts, and the inspirations of their visions. We absorb lessons learned and celebrate challenges overcome.

Because this movement is young, my research focuses on recent and contemporary case studies. However, these examples follow the groundbreaking work of Black congregations that decades ago invested to improve low-income areas around their churches through faith-based community development corporations and other methods. Their witness, legacy, and example of ingenuity and perseverance deserve our attention and teach us important lessons.

The Forerunners

In his book *Chaos or Community: Where Do We Go from Here?* Martin Luther King Jr. reported this:

> The assistant director of the Office of Economic Opportunity, Hyman Bookbinder, in a frank statement on December 29, 1966, declared that the long-range costs of adequately implementing programs to fight poverty, ignorance and slums (would) reach one trillion dollars. He was not awed or dismayed by this prospect but instead pointed out that the growth of the gross national product during the same period would make this expenditure comfortably possible. It is, he said, as simple as this: "The poor can stop being poor if the rich are willing to become even richer at a slower pace."[2]

Because so many of those with wealth can be slow to accept the kind of offer Bookbinder suggests, it sometimes takes the right idea to empower those at the grassroots level to take matters into their own hands. Faith-based community development corporations (CDCs) emerged as part of the civil rights movement in the late 1950s and '60s, taking shape and gaining momentum alongside the Great Society push of the Lyndon B. Johnson administration. King and social entrepreneur William H. Biddle, among others, championed CDCs for how they advanced economic empowerment at the local level in low-income neighborhoods.

Working through denominational structures or with individual congregations, these nonprofit organizations focused on the economic revival of neighborhoods closest to their founding churches. CDCs extended capital and capacity to create new businesses, commercial development, childcare, job training and placement, and, most of all, affordable housing. They sprang up in urban areas such as New York, Chicago, and Boston and also in rural areas serving immigrants and indigenous populations.

CDCs were seen as a complement to government programs in the 1960s and '70s. Millions of dollars flowed to CDCs through Community Development Block Grants, which were created in 1974, and later the Low-Income Housing Tax Credit, created in 1986. In subsequent years, these programs were cut back and replaced with nongovernment alternatives, such as the Local Initiatives Support Corporation (LISC) and the Enterprise Foundation.[3]

One of the most prominent of these alternatives, credited with leading the revitalization of Harlem, came out of Harlem's famed Abyssinian Baptist Church in 1989. Abyssinian Development Corporation focuses on providing quality affordable housing; delivering human services, particularly to the homeless, elderly, families, and children; fostering economic revitalization; enhancing educational opportunities for youth; and building community capacity through civic engagement. Its initiatives have added more than 1,244 housing units.[4]

A 1996 study found that about 14 percent of CDCs of all types are faith based.[5] Estimates of those specifically focused on housing are hard to find. Jill Suzanne Shook, founder of Pasadena Affordable Housing Alliance, notes that CDCs of all types created a quarter million jobs and more than a half million affordable housing units.[6] A range of other models of faith-based housing development followed the first generation of CDCs, each shaped to fit its own set of local factors, needs, opportunities, and challenges. But they all stand on the shoulders of the CDCs Black churches modeled years ago.

Apart from individual church CDCs, faith communities formed broader, formal alliances and networks to join forces and gain leverage. In 1981, for example, an interdenominational, interracial coalition took shape as the Nehemiah Plan in East Brooklyn, New York, to mitigate rising housing prices. By 1985, it had built 320 low-income homes. In Washington, DC, acclaimed real estate developer James Rouse helped fuel the creation of the Enterprise Development Corporation (later the Enterprise Foundation), which developed forty thousand low-income housing units with faith-based coalitions and other community-based nonprofits between 1981 and 1994. Nonprofit interfaith housing coalitions sprang up in Boston, Los Angeles, Philadelphia, Pittsburgh, San Diego, and St. Louis, as well as in smaller cities. Founded by Black pastors, the Washington (D.C.) Interfaith Network (WIN) became a coalition of fifty dues-paying congregations of all types. In Memphis, the Revelation Corporation, a joint venture of a mortgage company and five Black Baptist denominations, helped one thousand low-income families purchase homes and another four thousand obtain leases on affordable apartments.[7]

As federal housing policy shifted with each Congress and presidential administration, faith-based housing efforts ebbed and flowed but persevered, drawing on the model of the CDCs created in the 1960s.

The Big Picture

As today's congregations delve into issues and possible callings related to housing, each must balance its local context and community needs in a broader understanding of the options and alternatives. Housing experts and advocates often refer to a "continuum" or "spectrum" of types of affordable housing. It ranges from market-rate owner and rental housing to homeless shelters (see figure 1).

Figure 1

Graphic by Savannah Jillani.

Another way to assess need is a person-centered approach (see figure 2), considering the segments of the general population in need: working families and individuals, seniors and veterans, youths who age out of foster care, LGBTQ youth who have been rejected by their families, and those who need permanent supportive housing.

Figure 2

Graphic courtesy of Camoin Associates, camoinassociates.com[8]

As authors and researchers Gregg Colburn and Clayton Page Aldern write, America's homelessness crisis is really a housing problem.[9] There is not enough of any kind of housing, and the most vulnerable lose out. So what *are* churches doing in response?

St. Mark's Lutheran Church: Generations of Housing Ministries

Faith communities have taken many approaches to respond to their neighborhoods' needs. This book is spurred by a wave of recent examples. Some, however, have been at it for generations, rising to the call again and again.

In San Francisco, St. Mark's Lutheran Church stands as a model of congregational resourcefulness, welcome, long-term commitment, and entrepreneurial spirit. As one of the first Lutheran churches on the West Coast, St. Mark's draws on its sturdy German heritage. (It was known for decades as St. Markus Kirche, and services weren't offered in English until 1932.) Its grand sanctuary blends Gothic and Romanesque architecture and features a breathtaking rose window that has looked out over continuous neighborhood change since the church first came to be in 1862.

Few cities have faced the series of earthquakes and fires that have forced San Francisco to reinvent itself over and over again. It was, however, the convergence of two other powerful forces of the 1960s—urban renewal and a social-cultural revolution—that led St. Mark's to get into housing those in need. As in so many cities, sweeping highway construction in San Francisco displaced thousands of vulnerable residents. The new highways beckoned more-affluent city dwellers to depart for the suburbs. Many downtown churches followed, abandoning their original neighborhoods perhaps when they were most needed.

Rather than moving the church to the suburbs, however, the people of St. Mark's decided to stay put in downtown San Francisco. It was a heady decision. As city officials sought to reimagine what white flight and suburban sprawl left behind, the congregation was swept up in a redevelopment plan that spanned its surrounding sixty blocks. Virtually everything about its ministry context would change.

Seeing the need for safe, affordable housing in the heart of the city, St. Mark's took an active role in helping create the broader plan. It entered a partnership with the city government to build Martin Luther Tower, which offered modest rental rates for seniors with prescribed income levels. With 121 apartments, the thirteen-story tower was completed in 1962 and has become a familiar part of life on the church's campus.

It seems God was only getting started at St. Mark's. At about the same time, a handful of social service and religious leaders began to realize the growing need for outreach to those living on the streets and in the remaining, decaying, center-city housing stock. The city was attracting young people, who came seeking a fresh start in an alternative culture. Many were gay, lesbian, and queer long before America became more inclusive. The newcomers brought the wounds of being misunderstood or rejected outright—both back home and, sometimes, in their new city.

In 1962, a handful of pastors launched a night ministry to respond to whatever spiritual needs they encountered in their neighborhoods and beyond. Two pastors walked the streets at a time, meeting people where they were. One formative figure in that movement was Rev. Lyle Beckman. He recalls the start of the ministry in 1967 during the so-called Summer of Love: "The idea of the night ministry was to literally be on the streets of San Francisco and offer anything that might be needed in the moment. It could be a prayer. It could be a blessing. We thought we might have to be in crisis relief most of the time. But sometimes people just wanted to chat."

Beckman served as the city's "night minister" for fifteen years. His calm and approachable demeanor came in handy. More than once he found himself looking down the barrel of a gun held by an agitated neighbor. Mostly, however, he recalls simply extending the love of Christ that grounded his own faith. The ministry filled an unmet need on Sunday mornings. When churches didn't welcome the unhoused into worship, Beckman and others began offering "Open Cathedral"—outdoor church services in several parts of the city. Those services continue.

San Francisco, as almost all cities, fell behind in its efforts to address the affordable housing crisis. But with Martin Luther Tower as its new neighbor, the people of St. Mark's Lutheran created lasting and varied relationships with the residents, widening their understanding of what community can be. Some residents of the tower came to participate in life at St. Mark's, while others, including those who didn't come to worship, took part in a range of other ministries and activities. Using the church fellowship hall, Lutheran Social Services offered tower residents a range of activities, such as Tai Chi classes.

On my visit there in 2022, I learned that one day you may find residents stuffing candy in plastic Easter eggs before the annual community hunt. On another day, you may find St. Mark's members gathering with residents of Martin Luther Tower for lunch in the church fellowship hall to catch up on each other's lives. And as the plight of the unhoused grew in its city, so did the commitment of the St. Mark's flock. Beckman eventually came to serve as interim pastor, and the church began planning two more housing towers on its block, mixing income levels, populations, and ages.

Through the years, Beckman has observed how the relationship between the congregation and the tower residents has shifted in form and depth. St. Mark's has continued to adapt to using its spaces for activities with its on-campus neighbors and for the city, offering regular gatherings for fellowship and its stately sanctuary for concerts and other forms of the arts.

Beckman's vantage point combines his experience in street ministry with the more traditional duties of pastoring the largely white, affluent St. Mark's members, many of whom now live in the suburbs. So his voice in today's conversation about churches and housing rings with a unique authority. When it comes to whether a congregation should consider building housing, he cautions against assumptions and simple conclusions. Bringing people together across income ranges, neighborhoods, and life experiences yields many blessings. However, providing affordable housing on its expansive city-block property was never the church's strategy to grow membership, he says.

The authentic relationship-building required, however, takes sustained effort, energy, and vision through setbacks and interruptions due to the often-fragile lives of those who need affordable housing. "It's easy to say that we will be transformed," says Beckman. "That's a lofty goal. . . . Just know very clearly why you want to [build housing] in the first place. If it's just to make money, it's not going to work. If you think that automatically a hundred people will join your church, they are not necessarily. Will having housing on your property change the way the congregation lives its life? Maybe, maybe not. It can, absolutely. But there's got to be a strategy to make that connection."

On a summer weekday, tower residents and church members gathered to share lunch and life. There I met and interviewed St. Mark's member and retired banker Steve Ernst, who reflected on the church's ongoing journey in providing shelter. Even with the ups and downs from decades of experience, he said the congregation's calling to add more housing to the St. Mark's property is genuine. The new buildings will house an even more vulnerable population. But, he said, the members welcome the chance to deepen their faith and their call to service and hospitality.

"The congregation did a lot of introspection and had a lot of discussions," Ernst said. "We are making sure we believe we are continuing to fulfill the mission of the church. Now we will be taking care of a certain population that otherwise would be either unhoused or have difficulty finding a place."

The Crisis and the Movement Spread: First Presbyterian Church of Hayward

The same economic boom and neighborhood disruption that helped create San Francisco's housing crisis in the 1960s soon spread to other suburbs and nearby cities around Northern California. So did churches' efforts to use their properties to house their neighbors. Across California, faith-based organizations occupy 47,019 acres of potentially developable land, according to the Terner Center for Housing Innovation at the University of California, Berkeley.[10] California also forecasts the reordering of organized religion that is ahead for the nation. So we can look there for many other examples of how churches have responded to the housing crisis.

Located in the East Bay region, the city of Hayward is one of many suburbs that ring San Francisco and share in both its prosperity and its housing challenges. The First Presbyterian Church of Hayward (FirstPres) responded to its own deepening call to stand in the gap for the unhoused in the suburbs. The congregation's first step with offering seasonal shelter led to other steps—and, along the way, a revitalized and refocused congregation.

FirstPres's story echoes that of many congregations. The 125-year-old church grew steadily through the twentieth century as the town expanded, driven by the dual economic engines of agriculture and tourism. At its height, FirstPres counted about two thousand members before following a familiar pattern—white flight and church stagnation. The congregation is now smaller and more diverse. The membership of about 290 people has changed with its neighborhood, shifting from mostly white, middle and upper-middle class to a mix of Latino, Asian, and white members from a diversity of socioeconomic backgrounds and circumstances.

As the congregation and its context shifted, the church took time to discern new ministries and callings. Rev. Jake Medcalf, FirstPres's pastor, whom I interviewed in 2022, recounted how the church engaged local elected officials and neighborhood leaders in discussions about how the church could best help its neighborhood and city. The answer came loudly and clearly: help the unhoused. Local leaders were quick to refute the notion that the unhoused in Hayward had simply moved out from San Francisco. To the contrary, suburbs like Hayward are impacted by the same factors as the city—a preponderance of low-wage service-economy jobs, a shortage of housing overall, and, thus, a shortage of affordable housing and other shelter for the more vulnerable. In other words, those caught in Hayward's housing crisis are its own sons and daughters.

To see the crisis, the church looked no further than an encampment of the unhoused across the street from its own front doors. Its first step in serving these neighbors was to open a seasonal warming shelter in colder months. It grew into a year-round shelter and a day center where neighbors can charge their phones and access other resources.

"We asked ourselves, 'How does a congregation best use its resources?'" Medcalf recalled. "We had twenty-four thousand square feet of building space. We realized every unsheltered person needs a safe space to rest, read, charge a phone. We saw these ministries as an opportunity to build authentic relationships with those who came. We asked how we might help get our neighbors to the next step, whatever that might be."

After considering its abundance of space, the church partnered with Firm Foundation Homes to transform fourteen parking spaces into transitional housing in the form of tiny homes. (Tiny homes are independent, easily moved structures ranging from four hundred to one thousand square feet.) The congregation also deepened its study of the gospel and its commitment to the ministry of housing. Members grew in understanding Christ's call to serve those on the margins as well as in grasping the complexities of housing in America. Member and tiny home project leader Taryn Sandulyak said the journey was also deeply personal. "People had fears, questions, concerns, and gaps in awareness [about homelessness], and we had many conversations about those factors," said Sandulyak. "But I see former high school classmates on the street. . . . When you know someone's story, it's impossible to ignore them."

Along the way, Medcalf noted, congregation members learned they had to avoid the risks of "white saviorism," which combines white folks' sense of importance and self-satisfaction with a blindness for seeing and valuing those they serve as whole people, as children of God.

"You begin by feeling like I want to be the healer," he said. "But if I am constantly the healer and you are the sick, that perpetuates a toxic pattern. We learned that our unsheltered friends have gifts and skills that then became blessings to us as a community of believers."

"More than anything else, this is the church's issue to address," continued Medcalf, who, along with Sandulyak, later joined the staff of Firm Foundations. "The church is to take care of those who are suffering and to help people safely exist."

Garden Grove: The Church Not Ready to Give Up on Its Neighbors

Church-based housing initiatives are born of many different circumstances and motivations. Through more than 150 years of ministry, Garden Grove United Methodist Church saw its share of changes that have reshaped the American landscape and have shown where faith fits in. Those changes led to big decisions for the Garden Grove faithful.

Located south of Los Angeles, the city of Garden Grove grew from the construction of nearby Disneyland in the 1950s and '60s. The Mouse ate up thousands of acres of surrounding property—and along with it much of the area's housing stock. Because of the diminished supply, the remaining housing grew less and less affordable, especially for the workers who fueled the tourism economy Disneyland created.

Demographic shifts also reshaped the area and the Garden Grove UMC community. Over time, the congregation changed from white to multicultural. It came to blend newer Samoan- and

Vietnamese-American members with what remained of the white members, many of whom moved to neighborhoods farther away from the church. In time, United Methodist officials weighed their assessment of Garden Grove UMC's future and tagged it as a congregation that should be closed due to lack of vitality.

The remaining active members had another idea. Still energized by their mission and fellowship but with diminishing financial resources, they disagreed with their denominational leaders and voted to remain open, at least for a time. Their new goal was to create a legacy. Working with city officials, the congregation partnered with Jamboree Housing Corporation, a nonprofit housing developer founded in 1990. With an asset portfolio of more than $3 billion and experience creating nine thousand homes in more than eighty-eight California communities, Jamboree brought the expertise and development capacity Garden Grove UMC needed. In the summer of 2022, I sat down to hear the Garden Grove story from congregation member Wayne Sheriff, a retired insurance executive. He worked tirelessly to advance the church's alternative vision, one of life rather than death. "We decided we wanted to keep going, and we asked what that would take," recalls Sheriff. "We had a lot of conversations and came up with various ideas. One was to build this kind of concept."

The church dedicated half of its five-acre property to housing. It committed unused surface parking spaces and tore down part of an underused and aging education building, leaving ample parking and program space for the church's ongoing ministries. The church borrowed money from its endowment to engage legal representation—a critical element for any church doing housing, according to Sheriff. Funding came together from tax credits and local, state, and federal sources, and a bank provided $1.1 million in construction financing. Total development costs were $18.5 million. The congregation's contribution was its land, which it leased to Jamboree for sixty years and received about $600,000, including $200,000 up front. That cash relieved the congregation from immediate financial pressures and allowed it to refocus on mission and fellowship.

Jamboree manages the housing property, which carries the hearty Methodist name of Wesley Village and was completed in 2017. Its two three-story buildings create a multigenerational setting. The development includes forty-seven units of affordable housing for thirty-one working families and sixteen senior households and a recreation center, computer center, library, multipurpose rooms, laundry facilities, ten thousand square feet of open outdoor space with a patio, exercise equipment and seating, and covered and uncovered parking. Qualifying residents' annual income is between 30 percent and 60 percent of the area median, making Wesley Village a site of some of the most affordable housing in the Los Angeles region.

Jamboree's on-site manager, Benjamin Sanchez, says, "People came to this area for opportunity and a better life, but the cost of living is high. Just in this city we have families sleeping in hotel rooms five people to a bed. People like that needed something like this."

After opening Wesley Village, the congregation continued to worship, gather for fellowship, and host a Head Start program, which provides early education to children as well as health, nutrition, and parent-involvement services to low-income families.

"There was a lot of up-front discussion, and we worked to make sure everyone was signed on to this idea," Sheriff says. "We look at it as outreach. There was a need, and we were able to fill it. If we get church members from the residents there, that's fine. If not, that's fine too."

Whatever happens to the church, Sheriff says, its members know it has left a legacy. "The one thing we know is that we have done something for the community, let alone helping ourselves. We didn't just talk. We put our pedal to the metal."

Sheriff and the people of Garden Grove United Methodist speak for thousands of churches facing similar questions: How does an aging congregation with diminishing financial resources and uncertain long-term prospects carve out at least an interim future in which members can still worship and serve?

Hopes, Dreams, and Visions Spread

Clarendon Baptist Church Points the Way

Across the country, another epicenter of America's housing crisis is the Washington-Baltimore region. As in California, the area is home to a wide range of church-campus-based housing initiatives. One of the first was Clarendon Baptist Church in Arlington, Virginia, across the Potomac River from the nation's capital. Its example showed the way for other churches building housing in the Arlington area, and its story echoes that of other churches that once saw more materially prosperous days.

Opened in 1909, the once-rural congregation watched as Washington's growth swallowed and redefined Arlington as a suburb. In the 2000s, the church ventured forth into an example of housing that has inspired the region. The aging sanctuary, erected in 1950, was torn down. The church rebuilt a beautiful traditional sanctuary, a welcome hall, classrooms, and offices on the ground floor. Atop the church space is an eight-story apartment building. Of the apartments, 60 percent are designated as affordable housing for low-income tenants. The church steeple remains in place, a beacon that shows the building is a place of worship.[11]

Church of the Resurrection: An Easter Rebirth

Completed in 2012, Clarendon's early example soon spurred other mid-Atlantic congregations to pursue their own big dreams. Nearby, Arlington's Episcopal Church of the Resurrection followed and, in its own way, lived into its name. After decades of decline, the congregation redeveloped what was an imposing sanctuary built in 1964 sitting high on a ridge that overlooked its surroundings. Its new structure, named The Spire, offers smaller, better-suited worship space on the ground floor along with 113 units of affordable housing.

The church moved into its transformed campus on Easter Sunday 2021. On Sundays, about eighty people come for worship, in person and online, in three different worship services. They gather in the new, sunlight-bathed flexible space, recognized for its architectural beauty. The new sanctuary centers the cross that once sat atop the old steeple. The pipes of the same organ that once filled the former sanctuary now fill the new space with the same familiar and comforting embrace.

But there is far more at Church of the Resurrection that is new. The members of the reduced congregation now feel liberated from worrying about when the heating and cooling system will break again or how to pay the staff. Instead, they are channeling new energy and excitement toward mission outreach—feeding the hungry, caring for children, collaborating with other small congregations, and building community in multiple ways.

Getting to this new day hasn't been easy. In reimagining itself and its missions, the congregation was displaced for twenty-nine months, worshiping at a nearby seminary while its campus was remade. A preschool the church cherished had to be relocated, as did a food pantry. Some members with emotional attachment to the old buildings left. But new members have since joined, attracted by the congregation's missional passion, its new campus, and its COVID-necessitated online worship services, which continue.

The transformation began in 2013 when the congregation faced the question of whether it could regenerate itself by attracting new families with children. Members understood that aspiration would take years, if it could be achieved at all. In the meantime, it faced insurmountable campus maintenance and repair expenses. Members spent a year discussing and discerning a way forward. After helping start two nearby homeless shelters and participating in a collaborative effort to convert an existing apartment building into affordable housing in an increasingly unaffordable region, the congregation centered its energy on what else it could do to house its neighbors.

Working with Affordable Homes and Communities (AHC), a nonprofit housing developer, Church of the Resurrection spent two years refining its redevelopment plan. It focused on the housing needs of working families earning between 30 and 60 percent of the area median income. The church vestry (governing council) conducted congregational meetings throughout, which included several votes to adapt the project plan as it developed. Obtaining the necessary permissions, approvals, and construction permits took two years, reflecting both the complexity of church-housing initiatives and the congregation's perseverance.

With the appropriate approvals, the church agreed to lease its land to the developer for sixty-five years for $4.1 million. After clearing its property of the existing buildings to make way for the transformed campus, the church used some of that money to design and pay for new worship, program, office, and gathering space, which now sits alongside the new housing. The development cost $45 million. Funding came through a loan from the city of Alexandria, Low-Income Housing Tax Credits provided through the state of Virginia, private grants, and a conventional mortgage assumed by the developer. In the end, the congregation incurred no debt and emerged with operating spaces that fit its contemporary size and missions.

For the members of Church of the Resurrection, the season of campus redevelopment is behind them. It is a new day. Parking on Sundays is a little tight. Members and their families had to adjust when the construction design moved the memorial garden. But there is also new energy. Neighbors who once grumbled about the plan now delight in the sound of children playing on the playground of what was once a largely inactive church campus. As school children living in The Spire get off the school bus, they are met sometimes by congregation members, ice cream, and an invitation to story time. With operating costs greatly decreased, the church has funding for other community mission projects and passions.

Through it all, the congregation was indeed resurrected in its faith and its spirit, according to Kat Turner, the indefatigable member who championed the project and helped connect all the dots. Throughout the yearslong endeavor, the congregation wrote prayers for the project that were spoken each Sunday in worship. "We felt that our project responded to the commandment to love our neighbor," Kat says. "We also identified with the hymn 'All Are Welcome,' and its first verse":

> Let us build a house
> where love can dwell
> and all can safely live,
> a place where
> saints and children tell
> how hearts learn to forgive.
> Built of hopes and dreams and visions,
> rock of Faith and vault of grace;
> here the love of Christ shall end divisions:
> all are welcome; all are welcome;
> all are welcome in this place.[12]

Turner says the question of whether the church can achieve its hoped-for "regeneration" with young families remains open. The congregation is as active as before. Considering the move off campus followed by the pandemic, that is quite a statement. The long-term future of the congregation is unclear, which can be said about many churches. But for now, Turner says, the church is thriving, having been renewed and resurrected. "I think the people who stuck with us feel really good about where we are now as a church," she says. "We ended up saving ourselves but not quite in the way we thought we were going to save ourselves."

Turner observes that the congregation has a much stronger sense of identity and pride, especially because they had been through so much together. She notes, "Our mission was to create community with our neighbors, and we are still working to do that. . . . We offer what we can now and will leave behind a legacy regardless."

Housing for the Poorest amid the Richest: St. Paul's Episcopal Church

The Northern California suburb of Walnut Creek is an affluent feeder city to the region's booming tech industry. It's well connected to San Francisco by transit but far enough away to have its own charm—and its own housing crisis. Its affluence doesn't protect it from the widespread availability of methamphetamine that imprisons many who wind up living day-to-day on the streets.

The congregation of St. Paul's Episcopal Church has a long and distinguished history of service in Walnut Creek. In 1887, its first families purchased land on what is now Locust Street. The modest Carpenter Gothic–style chapel, built with sturdy local redwoods, opened the next year. It was moved in 1950 to the church's current campus on a tree-shaded ridge skirting the edge of the downtown area, now in the shadow of the Bay Area Rapid Transit stop that brings commuters to and from the city.

The church rode the wave of Christendom's heyday, growing significantly through the middle of the twentieth century. Now as a healthy faith community of about three hundred people with a church budget of about $600,000, St. Paul's came to its interest in housing through its own journey to understand housing and homelessness.

In the early 2000s, it launched the Fresh Start program on its campus to house respite and service programs for those experiencing homelessness or at risk of becoming unhoused. In 2012, that program merged with Trinity Center, a nonprofit organization offering complementary services and operating out of a home the church had purchased on an adjacent lot. The partners began to envision what would become a model of church-campus–based housing that is broader than any other I have found.

The outcome of this partnership centers housing and resources on those on the lowest rungs of the economic ladder. It includes a day center for the unhoused, called the Trinity Center, on the ground floor of a new apartment building, called St. Paul's Commons. In the Trinity Center, the unhoused can get out of the weather, charge their phones, do laundry, conduct research, receive services, and look to their next step. Above the Trinity Center, the apartment building offers forty-four units of permanent supportive housing (PSH) for those who have taken the next step.

PSH is an approach to housing those who have the most barriers to stability and independent living. It combines housing (long-term leasing or rental assistance) and supportive services. Those services can include childcare, housing search and counseling services, life skills training, mental health services, outpatient services, substance abuse treatment, and transportation.[13] The church partnered with Resources for Community Development (RCD), an affordable-housing developer with forty years of experience creating housing for low-income individuals and families. The partners engaged the John Stewart Company, a broad-based, long-standing multifamily development and property management firm, to manage the daily operations of the property. With all its services and amenities, St. Paul's Commons also attracted the interest of the Walnut Creek and Contra Costa County governments. As with other local governments nationwide struggling to identify new solutions to the housing crisis, they were eager to embrace out-of-the-box forms of partnership, even with houses of faith.

Primarily using the adjacent lot where it had previously purchased the single-family home, the church leased the ground to RCD for seventy-five years and has leased back a portion of the first floor for some church activities. The church does not receive any ongoing income from the apartments. Opened in 2020, the development provides homes for residents with incomes between 30 and 60 percent of the area median income, with 40 percent of the units set aside for residents with special needs or who have experienced homelessness. In addition, two units are dedicated to residents living with HIV or AIDS. Residents can receive services from RCD's resident services team as well as case management and free meals provided by Trinity Center.

Today the campus of St. Paul's hosts a range of activities: a preschool, worship, Sunday school, and other congregational activities, with church offices on one side of its modern sanctuary and Trinity Center and St. Paul's Commons on the other. Under the shade of a seventy-foot redwood, Trinity Center opens onto an outdoor plaza and seating areas covered by awnings. Unhoused neighbors gather for community and to take advantage of the center's services: showers, laundry, food, clothing distribution, and a shared kitchen.

Studio apartments about the size of a standard hotel room feature clean, sunlit spaces, each with a kitchenette. The building includes meeting rooms and ground-floor bike storage. A property manager lives on-site, and the main entrance is secured and monitored by the property management office next to the entry hallway.

More Than Bricks and Mortar: Learning to Be Neighbors

The St. Paul's story includes an important aspect of the church housing movement—how congregations prepare to be good neighbors to those who will live in the on-campus housing they build. As events turned out, residents of St. Paul's Commons moved into their apartments just as the congregation dispersed amid the height of the pandemic. It was bad luck for the congregation to acclimate to their new neighbors.

Rev. Krista Fregoso was called to serve as St. Paul's rector after the project was completed. When the pandemic eased, the congregation refocused on determining how to best help their neighbors without imposing. Fregoso realized that the foundational work to build the housing—financial, legal, and real estate development details—had been handled years earlier by a small circle of members who worked with the church's third-party partners. The congregation voted to donate the lot beside the sanctuary for the development. But, she notes, the project did not require a capital fundraising campaign or other formal commitment from the congregation.

In hindsight, Fregoso says, the congregation was not as fully educated and prepared for all the details and implications of welcoming the day center and housing onto its campus. Because the project was funded without the need for any up-front money from the congregation, the church missed an opportunity to build broad congregational awareness and understanding of its implications early on. Church members found they had to learn how to build relationships with their on-campus neighbors. Subsequent needs to raise additional funds provided another chance to fully educate the congregation.

"We have had some unexpected costs that required us to go back to the congregation for funding," Fregoso says. "Now we're hitting deeper and deeper layers of understanding. And now we [the church leaders] are saying, 'This *really* is what we are doing.' We're actively working to invite our neighbors into a deeper relationship."

As the Trinity Center serves those who are living on the streets, the church is learning each day, including how homelessness and mental illness often interact. "You just don't know what you are going to walk into each day," Fregoso says. "But it has opened up the congregation to say, 'Yes, there will be problems and we will work it through.' My hope is that the congregation will continue to open up and find a way to share in the lives of our neighbors."

How a Church Changed the Mind of the City Council: Fairfax Presbyterian Church

Back in Virginia, the members of Fairfax Presbyterian Church pursued their own vision of housing. In realizing it, they shaped local public policy to be more housing friendly and turned some neighbors' "Not in my backyard" to "Yes in God's backyard."

Fairfax Presbyterian's interest in housing sparked to life in the 1970s, when members called on landlords to address the poor housing conditions of local rental properties. That effort met some success.

But in the ensuing years, housing in Fairfax grew more unaffordable as the Washington metro exploded in size and affluence.

Fairfax next looked at what was literally its own "backyard," a peaceful, tree-shaded 8.26-acre property. Realizing it could rearrange some parking spaces to clear some of its land, the congregation agreed to help working families and, in a strategy rare among churches building housing, to create a way the residents could eventually own their homes. Church leaders wrote to the congregation, "As a church, we are taught to give our time, talent, and treasure to Christ. And treasure is not limited to money. Land ownership is one of the most valuable treasures within the City (and the County). Land is the treasure we can offer."

The church began discussions with two nonprofits, ultimately arriving at a vision of how to include both and address two types of housing needs at once. It worked with Homestretch, a thirty-year-old agency working to help homeless families become self-sufficient. A second partner was Habitat for Humanity of Northern Virginia, which would serve as the developer and build ten town-homes. Two would be reserved for Homestretch client families as transitional housing, and eight would go to families identified and prepared through Habitat to purchase their homes with low-interest loans and sweat equity. It was Habitat's first venture in Fairfax. The congregation launched a capital campaign that ultimately raised more than $500,000 to pay for the two Homestretch transitional homes.

National Capital Presbytery, the regional church governing body for Fairfax Presbyterian and a strong supporter of churches building housing, owns the land the church occupies. It leases a portion of the church property designated for affordable housing at one dollar per year. The church created a nonprofit corporation to serve as the leaseholder to sublease the land at a nominal fee to Habitat.[14]

But the dream still had to win approval from some skeptical city authorities who had the power to stop it. In the fall of 2022, the proposal came before the Fairfax Planning Commission. As Fairfax housing team member Peg Blomme recalls, a half dozen neighbors whose houses adjoined the church parking lot came to the meeting to speak against the project. They voiced concerns about the need to remove some trees to clear space for the homes as well as the added lighting the housing would bring. However, twice as many came to voice their support for the project. The planning commission voted to advance the proposal to the Fairfax City Council.

When the pivotal council meeting arrived, church leaders knew at least two members of the six-member council opposed the project. The partners presented the proposal, describing years of work and hundreds of hours of detailed planning and problem solving behind it. The Holy Spirit blew. After hearing the passion behind the vision, one of the council members who had expressed her opposition changed her mind on the spot and spoke enthusiastically in favor. Even the mayor, who rarely voted on matters, voiced his support for the vision. The proposal passed unanimously. The partners moved on to submit construction plans for approval, form the needed non-profit, arrange financing, and start construction.

"Since city council approved the plan, the pastor has spoken up more and more about housing as a ministry," Blomme says. "It's front of mind for him, and he wants to help spread this movement to other churches." Along the way, she adds, additional church members became active advocates for affordable housing and are now urging other congregations to look at their own backyards.

"The demographics of Fairfax are overwhelmingly upper class and white," Blomme says. "We felt the opposition [to more affordable housing] may grow, so we want to make hay while the sun shines. . . . We will go to other churches and say 'Hey, you've got land, and we can come to talk to you.' . . . It's about taking care of friends and neighbors. How can you not do that?"

How to Make One Plus One Equal Three: Friendship Presbyterian Church

On the northwest side of Chicago, as in so many other places, two historic Presbyterian churches had dwindled in membership and in their connection to their neighborhoods. They agreed to vacate their properties and say goodbye to their pastors, all to create something new—Friendship Presbyterian Church. The sales of the churches' properties generated about $4 million. After a large donation to its presbytery, Friendship invested the rest. The interest on the investments supplemented the new church's budget as it cultivated new life and energy.

With no property of its own for eight years, Friendship could relate, at least in part, to the experience of being rootless. For a season, members even worshiped in a transit station. They also invested time to learn the ways of community organizing, which a range of congregations have found to be well suited to understanding the needs and passions of a neighborhood. By listening to their neighbors first, rather than charging in with their own assumptions, they heard about issues of hunger, homelessness, and systemic racism. Friendship partnered with community leaders to form two advocacy groups, Neighbors for Affordable Housing and the Northwest Side Coalition against Racism and Hate. In an article profiling innovators in ministry, including Friendship's pastor, Rev. Shawna Bowman tells the rest of the story:

> In 2018, Friendship began collaborating with neighbors and with a not-for-profit affordable housing developer called Full Circle Communities to bring 75 units of affordable housing to the neighborhood. Through this partnership, Friendship developed a vision for a community center in the building, and when the building opened in April of 2022, Friendship Presbyterian moved in and launched a new not-for-profit called Friendship Community Place.
>
> Friendship Community Place is meant to be a space for conversations, collaborative programming, and convening resources that meet the needs of their neighbor in the building and in the wider community. They are committed to growing into this space at the pace it takes to create genuine relationships, and they are grounded in these values:
>
> • Collaboration and building relationships
> • Transformation and healing
> • Inclusion and belonging
> • Accessibility and solidarity
> • Nurture and sustainability
> • Risk-taking and celebration[15]

The new faith community embraced how "the hope and liberation of the Gospel is really good and really hard news." It learned how to build collective power to do the work of repair and restoration and, along the way, define itself as a community that seeks to replace its members' feelings of loneliness, fear, and oppression with creativity and community collaboration. "The Church is a beautiful, messy place filled with beautiful, messy humans capable of creating new ways of being and they're here for it."[16]

"It's Survival and Adaptation Pure and Simple":
Westminster Presbyterian Church

One of the most sweeping visions I found in my research is that of Westminster Presbyterian in Washington, DC, which I introduced in chapter 1. Westminster's story is yet another that is shaped by what urban renewal got wrong. Its neighborhood was one of the first in the United States to undergo urban renewal's insensitive destruction of an existing community, particularly its affordable housing, which reduced its supply of public housing by two-thirds to just twelve thousand units.

In trying to provide some of the feel of the suburbs, the redevelopment plan sought to create open spaces in the hope of keeping inner-city residents from moving out. The plan included closing streets and creating pocket parks. Along the way, the community lost its authentic sense of street life.

More recently, the city has reversed some of its errors and applied new planning approaches. But the neighborhood has suffered greatly. Several churches chose to remain in the historic neighborhood, and several are in various phases of redevelopment. However, Westminster's vision stands apart in how it begins with the needs of the community now, according to longtime pastor Rev. Brian Hamilton, who has lived in the neighborhood for two decades.

Partnering with Dante Partners and the District of Columbia, the church envisions two towers of affordable housing in a complex covering almost an entire city block. The first will be made up of 123 affordable apartments for active seniors aged fifty-five and older who make 50 percent or less of the area median income. Later the church plans a second tower of about a hundred apartments for families with incomes of 60 percent or less of the area median income. The ground floor of the first tower will include a flexible gathering space for worship and community events, exhibition space for neighborhood artists, and a recording studio to serve up-and-coming musicians. In 2022, the estimated cost was about $180 million.

Through music and the arts, the church envisions its new campus as a place of creativity and community, particularly for the neighborhood youth. The vision proclaims survival and renewal—for the neighborhood, for its young people, and for the church. Hamilton explains, "There is so much gun violence out there that the kids around here are literally dodging bullets. We have to change programming to engage the younger population. We need to put a community around them to show there is a different way of living a productive life."

Westminster had plenty of experience in playing the role of neighborhood pioneer. It welcomed and embraced the LGBTQ community before many others. Now its current vision is taking time to become reality. But the congregation isn't waiting for the project to be finished before adapting to its new calling. Members are already engaging in new forms of neighborhood outreach that fit the church's envisioned future, even as the campus transformation takes time to develop. As with other churches seeking transformation, it is listening first. Members have begun to collect oral histories from longtime neighborhood residents. "We are trying to do a lot of things that we can do anywhere," says Hamilton. "We know the transition will be hard, but we can't just stop. That winds up being dead air, and that's just not productive."

The congregation is also mindful that the new property will present a new set of demands on its pastoral leadership. As Hamilton reflects on near retirement, "I am telling the congregation they need to think of me as a transitional pastor. If the congregation is empowered and owns its new vision, then they will follow through with a new calling."

A Shift from "Serve Us" to Service: Central United Methodist Church

Each church I found that has built housing has done the work of excavation—digging up old ideas and dead traditions to make room for something new. In the case of Central United Methodist Church in Arlington, Virginia, their excavation was figurative and literal, and it led to all sorts of new discoveries.

Chartered in 1911, the church is located in the historic Ballston neighborhood of Arlington, where the prominent Ball family still casts a long shadow. At the turn of the nineteenth century, the family donated the land for the church (with the stipulation that it would be a whites-only congregation). The donation, however, came with a question of whether some members of the Ball family were still buried on adjoining land in a former family cemetery.

When the church decided to transform itself by tearing down all its buildings, historic preservationists swooped in and demanded that Central UMC confirm the bodies had been moved when the church was built in 1923. The dispute spread to a debate about how the church's proposed new building would sit alongside the former burial site.

The church had to adapt its original plan, which cost months of time, tens of thousands of dollars and, most poignantly, the loss of four thousand square feet of empty property, according to a church member who handled the negotiations. That four thousand square feet was the equivalent of six housing units in the church's plan. The delays, costs, and complications slowed but didn't stop this determined congregation. Central UMC persevered, drawing on decades of experience navigating change in its surroundings and context.

The church has stood for decades as Arlington has grown into a major suburb of Washington, DC. As with many others, it rode the wave of American Christendom up and then down. After decades of decline, at one of its moments of truth, church members took a walk around the neighborhood. It was 2007, and where a small country church had once stood alone they saw a busy urban block on a main road with a heavily used transit stop across the street. They also couldn't help but see how many of the church's neighbors experienced poverty and homelessness. Sensing a call, members began offering morning coffee and donuts to their neighbors. That grew into serving hot meals to hundreds. Over warm food and conversation, members came to know their neighbors, some of whom began attending worship services and taking part in church activities.

In 2014, the congregation formally expressed its dream to create new affordable housing on its property. That's when Rev. Sarah Harrison-McQueen was appointed senior pastor, with the charge to lead the church through the redevelopment process. She recalls, "They described themselves as a congregation that turned from facing inward to outward. They went from a 'serve us' perspective to a 'service' perspective, and that carried to thinking about the future."

As with many other churches with big housing dreams, Central UMC traveled a long and twisty road to a final design and vision. The first development partner withdrew. The congregation then joined with Arlington Partnership for Affordable Housing (APAH) on a revised vision. Then came the pandemic, which cost the church some of its active members who didn't return to church life when Central UMC eventually reopened. In fact, the challenges that came with the pandemic reoriented the congregation away from the old ways of being church and more toward mission and God's upside-down economics.

"Any congregation looking at doing something like this must have mission first and not money," Harrison-McQueen says. "If an economist looked at our situation, he would say sell all the land and move elsewhere to get the most bang for the buck. That might solve the issue of a crumbling building, but the real solution has to be mission driven."

In late 2023, the project partners completed an eight-story building that includes new functional space for Central UMC's ministries to the Arlington community. The 26,699 square feet of space the church occupies includes the sanctuary, offices, classrooms, a music suite, a commercial kitchen, and a fellowship hall. The new space also allowed for the expansion of the Kinhaven School, a preschool. According to APAH,

> The $84 million project secured 4% Low-Income Housing Tax Credits, low-cost loans from Virginia Housing and Virginia Department of Housing and Community Development (DHCD), in addition to CUMC's land lease proceeds, church fundraising, and financing provided by Truist Bank. The project [provides] 144 affordable apartments, including 15 units

reserved for very low-income residents earning 30% or less of the area median income (AMI), 60 units for those earning 50% AMI or less, and the remaining 69 at 60% AMI. It includes a mix of one-bedroom and larger, greatly needed, family-serving apartments including 24 two-bedroom units and 12 three-bedroom units.[17]

The congregation realizes the future of both the church and the neighborhood decades from now is beyond their seeing today. But it is newly energized and inspired. Instead of being so focused on its own existence, Harrison-McQueen says, the church is living into new understandings of what it means to be stewards of property in a community of need. Members also have a new understanding of what they can accomplish in following Christ's example of inclusion, sacrifice, and self-giving service.

"The word I would lift up for churches considering something like this is resiliency," she continues. "There have been so many challenges, but we knew that God gave us this dream and that one day it would be a reality. It's all about faith."

Autopsies or Revivals?: Fairlington Presbyterian Church

As churches emerged from the pandemic, author and church consultant Thom Ranier predicted that "church autopsies" would be a top trend in 2023. "Thousands of churches have closed, and we are trying to discover the reasons for their death," he wrote.[18] Ranier is correct. Many churches will take stock of their circumstances and face hard choices. Many will close. Some will dream new dreams. Either way, there is a lot at stake. As the congregations profiled in this chapter attest, callings to new life can defeat death when the faithful follow the ways of rebirth.

Witness Fairlington Presbyterian Church, another bunch of dreamers in northern Virginia. As the housing mission bug spread across congregations of all types in the mid-Atlantic region, the conversations about Fairlington's future were getting serious. It faced millions of dollars in repairs and a shrinking congregation. It looked across town at the examples of several of the pioneers in the movement. Fairlington had one eye on the inspiring examples of the housing other churches nearby had built on their campuses, and the other eye on its bank account.

The church's pastor, Rev. Juli Wilson-Black, recounts how the members of the session (the congregation's governing body) spent months considering the church's challenges and asking themselves hard questions about its future. In being honest with themselves, the leaders found the courage of their faith as a source of strength over their fears. "We were looking just at the numbers and saying to ourselves, 'Shoot, this church is not going to be around in a decade if we don't do something now,'" Wilson-Black recalls. "But as we continued to talk about it, the conversation shifted from being about survival to being about mission. Some sense of urgency is helpful, but you can't let the urgency drive the decision."

In the fall of 2022, Fairlington marked its seventy-fifth anniversary as an entirely new day for the church and the community. Realizing it didn't need all the parking spaces it once required, the congregation decided to sell its excess property to Wesley Housing. Wesley built a new community called The Waypoint, offering eighty-one apartments of various sizes and below-market rental rates, none more than 60 percent of the area median income.[19]

With the income from the sale of its parking lot land, the congregation addressed some much-needed repairs to the church buildings and sanctuary. It also funded a new staff member charged with community outreach. The congregation is reenergized and refocused not just on how to build relationships with its new neighboring apartment dwellers but also the broader community. The transformation also reminded the congregation of its reason for existing.

"Above and beyond the housing, what this effort has done is give us a much greater clarity around why the church is here," Wilson-Black reflects. "It's very clear to our people now that God has called us to be a blessing to our neighborhood and that there is a very direct connection. The litmus test we are using is, 'Is the neighborhood better off because we are here?'"

Fairlington is a testament to what a small congregation can do. By the end of 2022, there were eighty-three members on the roll, close to the average size for mainline Christian congregations in the United States. But there is nothing common about Fairlington's journey and its testimony. The members of Fairlington are changing the conversation about "church revitalization."

Thinking about the pressures facing almost all small churches, Wilson-Black recounts what is often said but adds an update for her flock: "Churches say, 'We need more members because we need more money because we need more people to help.' Now Fairlington members are saying, 'We want more members because we are so excited and more people need to know that the church can be this kind of community—open, inclusive, loving, and reaching out to neighbors.'" Wilson-Black sees every day that Fairlington now has new energy and capacity to evangelize and share the good news of God's Easter story, of resurrection.

"Like a Spring of Water"

To repurpose God's land and properties, to reawaken their sense of calling and relevance, to create welcoming, inclusive communities that bear witness to God's vision of shalom. To face and overcome neighborhood opposition. To shape the workings of government. To muster the courage to listen and respond to an altogether new call, especially when the way forward is not guaranteed. None of it is easy or for the fainthearted. But these and other stories demonstrate how ordinary people can do extraordinary things when they grasp a vision and act with faith. Everywhere I looked, I saw these distinct, creative, and context-tailored examples of this growing movement.

College Park (Georgia) United Methodist Church, chartered at the turn of the twentieth century, faced a shrinking congregation and $1.5 million in deferred maintenance expenses on its campus. But it owned a parking lot next to a rapid transit stop as well as an underused education building. The church partnered with Tapestry Development Group to build fifty apartments for those at 60 percent of area median income as well as ten units at market rate. In addition, it partnered with Good Places, a consultant that works with churches to reimagine their property, to convert the church's education building into sixteen live-work lofts aimed at artists. The condos sell in a range from $155,280 to $195,900, with a monthly homeowners' association fee of $200.

In downtown Atlanta, the historic First United Methodist Church retained its classic sanctuary and used the balance of its land to make way for a two-tower complex design offering more than three hundred one-, two-, and three-bedroom apartments, 85 percent of which will be affordable. The new space also houses the Atlanta First Day School, a pre-K and K–5 private school operated by the church, as well as a new fellowship hall, gymnasium, church classroom space, and administrative offices. The site includes a commercial component—ten thousand square feet of retail space—as well as 260 parking spaces.

In downtown Denver, St. John's Cathedral (Episcopal) offered a parking lot to create fifty affordable, permanent supportive housing apartments that opened in 2018. St. Francis Center, which serves the unhoused, helped fund the project through private donations and $8.5 million in Low-Income Housing Tax Credits. The church has leased the land to the nonprofit for one dollar per year for at least fifty-five years.

In their own ways, a number of smaller churches have also demonstrated ingenuity and generosity in helping to house their neighbors:[20]

1. Mosaic Christian Community (Church of the Nazarene) is an energetic, multiethnic church on the east side of St. Paul, Minnesota, that has developed a village, called "Sacred Settlement," of six tiny homes on its property. Four homes are for people coming out of homelessness, and two are for people who have not experienced homelessness and are dedicated to living a life in community, offering their experiences, knowledge, and support. The church building functions as a common house and includes a kitchen, a shower room, and social areas.
2. IKAR, a Jewish community in West Los Angeles, included sixty apartments in building its new campus, which also includes a new synagogue and preschool. IKAR selected the Community Corporation of Santa Monica to build and manage permanent

supportive housing for formerly unhoused seniors. In addition to housing, there will be essential supportive services on-site.

3. First Christian Church of Tacoma, Washington, is a small church generously hosting a village of thirty-nine tiny homes that provide transitional housing. The church also hosts a community kitchen, a hygiene trailer with restrooms, showers, and laundry facilities, staff offices, and a security pavilion. There is 24/7 staffing and case management on-site to help residents explore housing, employment, health care, education, and other services.

4. In Portland, Oregon, Hillsdale Community Church was once a flourishing congregation of more than five hundred. Now with fewer than one hundred members, it is entering a process of repurposing its land and buildings and earnestly exploring models for hosting housing for those who would otherwise be unsheltered.

5. Glencliff United Methodist Church in Nashville hosts a village of homes focusing on people needing short-term medical care. Caregivers or children can be included. On-site medical assistance and three meals are provided each day.

6. Genesis Worship Center in Oakland, California, is an independent, Black-led congregation launched in 2003 that hosts twelve apartment on its property, made possible through a mix of creative financing, collaborations, and adaptive reuse of existing space.

In these and other places, congregations are demonstrating the audacity of their faith and changing their communities in ways they never have before and perhaps never thought they could. Some feel the rejuvenation of new purpose and are thriving in new ways. Some have rediscovered why the church exists. Some are writing new chapters about what church revitalization can look like. Others may still acknowledge that the end of their life together may be near, but they know they have invested themselves and God's resources to leave lasting legacies, created communities that are more deeply connected, and built stable places that will affect thousands of lives over time. Each in their own ways and in their own contexts, they have lived into the words of the prophet Isaiah:

The LORD will guide you continually
    and satisfy your needs in parched places
    and make your bones strong,
and you shall be like a watered garden,
    like a spring of water
    whose waters never fail.
Your ancient ruins shall be rebuilt;
    you shall raise up the foundations of many generations;
you shall be called the repairer of the breach,
    the restorer of streets to live in.

                                                  Isa. 58:11–12

Chapter Six

Board by Board, Brick
by Brick, Home by Home

Lessons and Learnings

Unless the LORD builds the house,
those who build it labor in vain.

Ps. 127:1

A church that is indifferent to poverty, or evades responsibility in economic affairs, or is open to one social class only,
or expects gratitude for its beneficence makes a mockery of
reconciliation and offers no acceptable worship to God.
The Confession of 1967, in *The Constitution of the Presbyterian
Church (U.S.A.)*, Part I, *Book of Confessions*, 9.46

For all their abundance, America and its churches know a mani-
fold poverty.

First, every American town and city is touched by a poverty of housing that affects not just the housing-starved but the soul of the entire
community. We do not have nearly enough safe and affordable housing for our neighbors with middle and lower incomes, and, as with
most things in America, Black and Brown people are disproportionately targeted and harmed by this crisis. Second, America suffers from
a poverty of community—the capacity to create spaces where those
of intersecting backgrounds, beliefs, identity expressions, and income
levels live together in everyday proximity, in peace, mutual respect,
and support. Too many have retreated to political, ideological, and

125

socioeconomic extremes and reinforce our divisions by living in separated neighborhoods and housing types. Third, churches built for the peak of American Christianity face a poverty (at least a worldly one compared to prior times) of what they once had—a wealth of members and money. Under the pressure of shrinking resources, some churches face a poverty of missional imagination. What isn't lacking around them is deep human need, both spiritual and material, and the ever-surprising abundance we can find in the Lord.

In prior chapters, we examined the convergence of these three crises and the emerging movement of churches responding with their land, their buildings, their hearts, and their faith. The movement's sustainability isn't certain. An abundance of questions and tests remain before we know whether this is a viable response to our national polycrisis.

This chapter holds that movement up to the light. I draw on my congregation's ten-year journey to create on-campus housing, the dozens of case studies I've researched, and my personal experience in forty years of watching and participating in the housing conversation in Charlotte. I should add that while I've examined the housing crisis at a moment when it is particularly tight, it will fluctuate. One day's demand-driven high prices and rents may be the next day's buyers' and renters' market. Those fluctuations do not dismiss the deep, structural realities that form the heart of the housing crisis. Below-market housing is harder to build and less profitable for those who do build it, meaning it will always be passed by for those looking just to make money. The consensus among experts is that the housing crisis took decades to create and will take just as long to fix. How and whether America responds to fix it remains to be seen.

In the introduction to the 2023 National Low Income Housing Coalition report, the Congressional Caucus on Homelessness describes the challenge this way:

> There is a crisis in our nation: millions of people across the country are without a home or are struggling to keep a roof over their heads. We see homelessness and housing instability in every community in every state. Far too many people have lost

their homes to high rents and evictions, with nowhere to turn but cars, shelters, or the street. And millions more are at risk.[1]

People of faith bring their own lens to these challenges. We recall how God gathered the children of Israel on the banks of the River Jordan after their liberation from bondage and difficult trek through the wilderness. As they looked out on the promised land, God sat them down for a long talk about their responsibilities to use the land for the benefit of all. Reflecting on this scene, Walter Brueggemann writes, "Land brings responsibility. It is a radical idea challenging our usual notions of possessions, for we think much possession make one immune from caring." He continues: "Only the landed are tempted to forget."[2]

As powerfully as our faith may call us to intervene to extend the love and justice of Jesus Christ, history speaks soberly about the mixed track record of churches that jump into housing. Author and Princeton sociology professor Robert Wuthnow concludes that faith communities have historically faced "a vortex of competing interests from developers, employers, homeowners, advocates for open land and sustainable energy, and advocates for economic growth and low taxes."[3] In his thoughtful review of the faith communities' efforts in housing from the 1960s to 2023, he writes:

> The faith communities and community development organizations that made a dent in the demand for affordable housing were sufficiently motivated to figure out how to work around the complexities of these constraints. It was a daunting endeavor, but one that could sometimes succeed when congregations participated with coalitions with sufficient resources and expertise.[4]

So where does that leave us today and this newest form of a church housing movement? What questions fit today for people of faith? What has America forgotten? How are its churches invited to pause, listen, and remember our covenant obligations? How are we to prayerfully and deeply discern our role?

And what about "community"? Is the idea of building housing on church property really a way to create community? Yes, as we are all looking for a "home" of the same kind. Kevin Nye, who worked among the unhoused in Los Angeles, says, "However crucial the role of housing in ending homelessness, we cannot forget that experience of being *home*less also means a lack of many of the things we associate with 'home,' things as indispensable as safety, belonging, dignity, and hope."[5]

Safety. Belonging. Dignity. Hope. Aren't these the real things of community? Doesn't our sovereign God shape us to thrive on these things? Aren't they for all of us, including our unhoused neighbors? *Meaning. Calling. Purpose. Trying hard things. Growing.* Aren't these the things we *all* need in life? Aren't they what we need to climb out of our fearful, self-possessed, myopic bubbles to cross and fill the gaps that divide us into haves and have-nots, housed and unhoused, old and young, and across so many other aspects of our beloved createdness?

Safety, belonging, dignity, hope, meaning, calling, purpose, trying hard things, growing—these are the building blocks of real community and of God's church as a home to all. Aren't these the things of resurrection and new life, once we die to living just for ourselves? What might be the blueprints for that kind of community?

Discernment: Bound to Fail without God

> Make me to know your ways, O LORD;
>   teach me your paths.
>
> Ps. 25:4

The congregations that helped with my research have used the words above, or something like them, as they have sought the way of the Lord. Some have prayed from a position of abundance, others at a crossroads in the life of their congregation, still others with only months to go before running out of money and members. All began with prayer, including the faithful of downtown Atlanta's First United Methodist Church.

"The church had retreated inward, and we were trying to turn back out," Rev. Jasmine Smothers recalled. "Several people on the streets had died on our front steps, including one who was murdered. The congregation said, 'We can't just stand by anymore.' We did a visioning series and began to consider dreams that were so big that, without God, they were bound to fail."[6]

In all things, begin with prayer.

What follows prayer? Here are some of the other building blocks of faithful visioning:

1. **Community and context.** Take a fresh look at the church's mission field and ask questions like these: What breaks God's heart? What is the history of your community? Who has been displaced, excluded, overlooked? Who is suffering, vulnerable, powerless, underserved? What is the history of the church? Has it done harm to others in its community that needs repair? What is the church's passion? What population is the church called to serve—seniors, veterans, families, those with disabilities, the LGBTQ community, youths aging out of foster housing, those who are reentering the community from incarceration? What services currently exist for those in need? Is there a gap the church can help fill, one that no one else will step up to address?

2. **Assets, resources, strengths, and weaknesses.** What resources does the congregation have to offer? Land, excess parking, unused or underused buildings, financial resources? What professional skills and lived experiences do church members have that can be harnessed? Does the church have social capital on which to draw—connections that can help it learn about its community's housing needs and respond with land, money, partnership, or something else? As important, does the church have the stamina for what will inevitably be a years-long and, at times, arduous undertaking? What blind spots might limit its vision? What shortages—resources, people, energy, agreement—might hinder a big undertaking? Can they be overcome?

3. **Neighborhood.** What connects the church to its immediate neighbors and neighborhood? Does the church have insights into how its neighbors would receive the idea of housing (or any other bold public witness)? How many members live near the church? How many live in other parts of town, and how might that matter? Who will advocate for the church's vision, and

who won't? How can the church turn "Not in my backyard" (NIMBY) into "Yes in God's backyard" (YIGBY)?

4. **Government and public policy.** Is local government focused on affordable housing? If so, how? What initiatives has it launched and why? Has it considered houses of faith as part of the solution? What financial resources are available through national, state, and local governments? How is your land zoned, and would that have to be changed? What's involved in changing zoning if that's needed?

5. **Partners and partnerships.** What nonprofit organizations currently serve those in need of affordable housing in your community? What do they offer, and how do they work together? Talk to their leaders at length! Listen to their ideas about where there are gaps, hurdles, and opportunities.

These are just some of the categories of discernment—and they are only a start. Even after Caldwell Presbyterian, the church I pastor, decided we wanted to explore using our building for housing, a specifically appointed vision team took another year to interview local experts and leaders, both grassroots and high-level public officials, to research the community's needs and the possibilities for our building, land, and neighborhood. Most important, this "dream team" took its time to try to include as many voices and perspectives as possible—both internal and external to our community of faith.

Finally, understand that any initial vision will change over time as hurdles, roadblocks, and new learning and information arise. Pay attention to who in the congregation is energized and called to the vision and who isn't. Use that as an initial gauge for your church's capacity and leadership for a big but transformative undertaking.

Assembling the Project Team

Every church interviewed or researched for this book testified to the importance of gathering the right leaders and professionals, from inside the church and beyond, once a project has been sketched out. Pastors and church people are often not equipped with the technical, business, and other skills that will be needed. A gap in a project team can lead to big problems during and after the project is undertaken. Here are some key roles and members:

1. **Laity/membership.** A range of congregational perspectives can ensure a balanced consideration of the "how," the "what," and the "whether" in a congregation's thinking, planning, and praying. Any team should include those with clear vision, leadership, energy, endurance, and respect from within the congregation, including those who represent the flock overall. Members can also bring the needed ability to communicate the status and issues related to the initiative (using town hall dialogues, online media channels, words, and visuals). Obviously, a strong link and regular reporting relationship to the church's governing body (board of deacons, session, etc.) is critical. Churches are well suited to find direct or indirect expertise, wherever possible, in areas such as real estate and development, banking and finance, and the church's existing and potential new mission capacity, interest, and focus.

2. **Legal.** A church member with a legal background is helpful. Ultimately, however, every project needs objective legal counsel and advice that holds the church's best interests in mind at all points in the journey.

3. **Social support services.** Whether through a church member or a committee member at large, churches should also involve someone with knowledge of the needed services for different marginalized populations.

4. **Financial.** Housing initiatives are very complex financially. As with legal counsel, objective, third-party financial advice and guidance should be involved early on. Keep in mind that each project has two phases, each with its own particulars—construction and operation.

5. **Community connection.** Every team needs people with professional experience in the nonprofit, social work, grassroots organization, or affordable housing fields. These people will connect the project team to the ongoing needs, gaps, and developments in the community beyond the congregation and its neighborhood, especially the nonprofits focused on the

population the church chooses to house. The more combinations of those perspectives, the better.

6. **Lived experience.** It is easy to leave out people who can sit in on your planning to bring the voice of those whom you hope to serve. Without that perspective, it is easy (if not likely) for those of us who come from perspectives of privilege and/or whiteness to get it wrong. If the congregation intends to live in close relationship and proximity to its new on-campus neighbors (or if it just wants to understand the experience of being unsheltered), those with lived experience of homelessness or some form of low-income, subsidized, or affordable housing can provide critical learning and valued knowledge. As important, they should be compensated justly because their lived experience is uniquely valuable and is to be valued.

7. **Neighborhood relations.** The planning team will also benefit from having members who live in the surrounding neighborhood or at least are engaged from time to time. Also, include nonmember neighbors who might participate as friendly ears and voices of the neighborhood. While care, trust, and discretion are needed, this can avoid miscommunication or other surprises that can derail the project down the track.

8. **Architect.** The advice, counsel, vision, and technical skills of a good architect can be underrecognized by the average church member, especially on the front end. But the sooner an architect can be engaged, the better. An architect can help the congregation dream and imagine and can protect the church's best interests in the design and construction phases of the project.

Choosing a Good Partner: the Developer

Of singular importance to every project is the church's choice of a developer. The developer takes the lead on the real estate–related aspects and guides the congregation's choice of the type of housing to build. The developer navigates the project through local government, zoning and land-use issues; identifies and marshals sources of funding; and works with the church to envision an ongoing, financially sustainable community after neighbors move in.

In most cases, the developer brings in the architectural, civil engineering, and general contracting teams needed. With new multifamily (apartment) or adaptive reuse projects, the developer often becomes the church's ownership partner for at least the initial years of the community's operations.

The supply and availability of the right kind of developers are the keys to how this movement will spread. By "right kind," I mean developers with experience, patience, knowledge, and aptitude to work with churches, most of which know very little of what is involved or needed. In cities and communities with multiple developers who "speak church," projects thrive and proliferate. Where there is a shortage of church-friendly developers, congregations are left with few ways to get things going. The number of church-housing projects in California, the mid-Atlantic, and New York City, for example, directly reflects the range of developers who can successfully work with churches.

The fit between the church and the developer is crucial. Each project has its own twists, turns, frustrations, disappointments, reconsiderations, and renegotiations. Each also has its victories and celebrations. For various reasons, more than a few of the projects I researched changed developers midstream.

For all these reasons, churches should consider hiring an "owner representative" as an adviser in working with the developer and other partners. These professionals bring knowledge of real estate development that churches usually lack. They hold the church's best interests at heart and can be contracted for various stages of a project, working on an hourly basis or through a defined phase of the initiative—from preliminary dreaming to project conclusion.

There are both for-profit and nonprofit developers and advisory firms in markets where this movement is emerging—places like Seattle, Atlanta, San Francisco, Los Angeles, the mid-Atlantic, and Charlotte, among others. If, for instance, there were more in a place like Charlotte, I suspect more churches would be further along in their dreams and planning. While the church-housing movement has always been most evident in urban areas, that may change in the coming years. Small and rural churches face unprecedented if not existential challenges as Christianity and organized religion face the coming transformation, whatever shape it takes. While church housing is not a nonissue for smaller, rural churches in the years to come, their success in the movement will require denominational vision and expertise, the partnership of enlightened and ready public and elected officials, and the help of financial institutions, even as more and more are withdrawing from smaller markets.

Pastoral Leadership

The church housing movement places unique importance on clergy and other pastoral leaders for both traditional and new roles. Theological, biblical, and pastoral insights frame the work of the project team and keep it grounded. The team will inevitably need pastoral care as the project goes through victories, setbacks, and disappointments in its evolution. The pastor occupies a unique role in casting a vision for housing that the entire congregation can embrace. The best, most regular chance to do that is in worship, through the Word read and proclaimed, the sacraments celebrated, and prayers offered and requested at every step.

But a clergyperson must be far more than a priest to the project team, a Sunday school teacher, and a biblical interpreter of how God calls us to love our neighbor. After working with a range of churches that are creating on-campus housing, Rev. Heidi Worthen Gamble, Pacific Presbytery Mission Catalyst for metro Los Angeles, believes the movement calls for a new kind of pastoral leadership. "Pastors must build up the core leaders from within the church. Their buy-in is essential," she says. "But the projects require a pastor to have much more—chutzpah, a strong motivational drive, flexibility, adaptability, and savvy."

Because membership in the project leadership team may change through the yearslong process, Worthen Gamble says it often falls to pastors to provide the consistent, steady leadership that congregations need to persevere: "Pastors must have a lot of emotional maturity to see it through. We need pastors who see learning new skills as a joyful challenge, who don't get easily discouraged, and who are willing to turn on a dime as project visions change. . . .

And it's not about size. I've seen small churches with strong leadership do amazing things. You can have a church of forty people be successful."

Clergy leaders also need to be deeply plugged into their community, veterans of the movement say. Their trustworthiness and credibility, or lack of it, affect how the church's neighbors and surrounding area view a housing initiative and whether they will oppose it or support it. To help pastors build these skills, Pacific Presbytery offers regular learning opportunities for clergy to study real estate, development, and other technical aspects a project will entail. Pacific also has informal learning networks among its member churches, because, Worthen Gamble says, a church should not try to do a project on its own.

The LA Voice, a multifaith organizing group in Southern California, uses community organizing principles to build advocacy and to connect clergy and congregations that are involved in housing issues and development projects. "It's very easy for churches to be bullied by developers," Worthen Gamble says. "LA Voice plays a middle role between congregations and the other parties involved."

Pastors and congregations that understand and use the principles of community organizing—fostering relationships, achieving consensus, and building grassroots power—are often the best equipped. "Congregations need to be open and able to understand and build relationships with the neighborhood," Worthen Gamble explains. "That doesn't mean that all the neighbors have to be on board. But it does sometimes mean going door-to-door and listening to concerns. We want the neighborhood to say, 'Thank God for that church. They are doing what is important.'"

Funding, Finance, Ownership, and Operations

Money makes or breaks any endeavor at any stage. No project gains momentum without some sort of seed funding to cover the costs of initial fact-finding and exploration. This might be to hire a consultant to guide a church with initial steps, a lawyer, or an engineering firm to assess whether a building could be adapted for housing (as in the case of Caldwell's Easter's Home project). Other seed funding can hire grant writers to find the money for continued exploration.

If land is involved, up-to-date surveys will be needed to confirm its boundaries and ownership. Lawyers may need to be hired to advise on zoning or up-front policy issues. A developer will not go too far in exploring a project without some form of payment arrangement. For example, Caldwell initially worked with its developer, Dream-Key, through a memorandum of understanding until the project was legally closed and finished, when we entered a far more detailed partnership agreement.

If the church does not have such exploratory capital and cannot raise it from the congregation, this kind of "dream" funding isn't always easy to find, but it does exist. Sources may include local philanthropic organizations, family foundations, state or local government, and nonprofit agencies. In a few cases, a church's ecclesiastical body, such as a diocese, presbytery, synod, or conference might offer exploration grants.

Structure and Ownership

A central question to be addressed early will be the structure of the venture. Will the church sell the land needed? Will it be paid in a lump sum or over time? Or will the church offer a long-term lease for the land and receive ongoing income from the project (if income is needed)?

In turn, that question raises the need for clarity about who owns the church land. Baptist churches usually own their own land in some form. In other Protestant denominations, the ownership of church land varies. Often the land occupied by churches in the Presbyterian Church (U.S.A.) and other branches of Presbyterianism is entrusted to the congregation but is owned by the presbytery.

In Caldwell's case, the presbytery owned the land entrusted to Caldwell. For a symbolic, nominal amount, Caldwell leased the land under the building that we adapted into housing for the specific purpose of affordable housing for fifty years. That required full floor approval at a meeting of representatives of our region's more than ninety congregations. As an apartment building, Easter's Home will operate as a limited liability company jointly owned by Caldwell and its development partner, DreamKey Partners. Caldwell will receive no income from Easter's Home.

Other ecclesiastical bodies present their own structures and need for permissions, approvals, and so on. These approval processes alone have taken months or even years in some cases. So the earlier a congregation understands them, the better.

Some churches choose to be co-owner in the finished project. This can provide an ongoing revenue stream. As important, it can ensure that the church has some voice in the governance, values, and operations of the housing community.

As these stories show, there is a range of approaches. Churches that use open parking spaces for tiny homes or donate church land to build for-sale, affordable housing on their campus will face other sets of issues.

Operations

Once a congregation has identified which type of population it wants to house, it must find the right operating partner. The operating-partner role includes managing the tenant selection and handling leasing, rental payments, and other aspects of being in the rental property business. When public funds are used, they can come with compliance-reporting requirements. As with developers that "speak church," the proximity of community agencies and other homelessness and affordable-housing service partners affects how this movement spreads.

Housing is just the start. Congregations should remember they lack the social work background needed to know how to best support those in affordable housing. An operating partner brings that knowledge. Professional case management is essential to a range of models of housing for marginalized or at-risk populations.

When the housing is on church property, however large or small, the congregation relies on the relationship with the housing community to be intimate and fluid. The agreement between the church and the operating partner will need to be comprehensive, transparent in detail, and seamless in execution. What values inform the members' desire to help? Where does the church's heart lie relative to the type of population it really wants to serve?

Separate from managing the services a given population needs, the building itself also brings requirements. Who will manage the property, and how will that entity be paid? Upkeep and appearance of affordable housing will be a source of both congregational and neighborhood concern before and after the residents arrive. Property management is also a critical financial issue. Congregations will need to explore who the property managers are that work in the area, as well as their costs, standards, and reputations.

Operational Funding and Financials

The funding of housing projects is complex, to say the least. These considerations require the capacity to bring a commitment to God's values and economics to the table and—just as important—careful, dispassionate financial consideration to avoid failure down the road.

Churches generally break down their projects into two phases. The first is construction. What type of housing will be built? Will it be new construction or adaptive reuse of an existing building? For-sale housing or something else? Adaptive reuse of existing buildings brings its own trade-offs. It preserves existing, sometimes historic structures and is gentler on the environment but is usually more expensive and often more time-consuming than new construction.

Will the project require long-term debt? How will that debt service affect the rental income that is needed and, therefore, the monthly rental rates to be charged? For example, in Caldwell's case, we worked very hard to avoid debt beyond the construction phase. This allowed us to serve those with low and very-low incomes—30 percent to 50 percent of the area median income.

Who will choose the architect and the general contractor to design and build the housing? Will those entities be hired by—and responsible to—the developer or the church? In most cases the answer is the developer, whose business is to oversee and manage these aspects.

These details require very specific experience and skills. They can be time-consuming and exhausting. Again, the church should consider hiring an "owner representative" with real estate financing and development experience to represent its best interests. However amicable the relationship with the developer is, an owner representative is needed as a third-party to advocate for and protect the church through every phase of the project's development and execution.

To pay for construction, a combination of funding and financing solutions is usually needed. Most often the developer identifies and obtains the funding with the church's input and partnership. Funding from federal, state, and local sources may also be available. (See appendix C for details on Caldwell's construction and development funding mix, as one example.) Each source of public funds is created to achieve certain public interest goals and help different subsets of people. That includes veterans, those living with HIV, seniors, those living with a range of disabilities, those who have been chronically homeless, and others. Each public source also comes with its own set of reporting and compliance requirements that must be tracked and met.

Once a building is financed and constructed, a church and its partners must focus on the finances of the ongoing operation, which involves a detailed understanding of income, expenses, and maintenance of the building. The sheer complexity of the design and construction phases can distract congregations from focusing on the operational viability of an initiative. Many projects involve federal subsidies that close the gap between what the renter can afford to pay and the actual full rental rate. Some churches, however, deliberately avoid public funding because of the "strings attached" or out of an ideological principle.

Federal funding is given to local governments to distribute through programs such as the Low-Income Housing Tax Credit. Congregations and their partners need to understand the "upstream" source of construction funding and public rental subsidies. No government funding is guaranteed forever. How important is public funding to the ongoing income of the property, and how durable and predictable is it? Has it proven to be politically popular and accepted over time, or is it vulnerable to shifting political winds? How long has that source existed? How easily might it end with a change in Congress or your state legislature?

Navigating NIMBYSM, Shaping Public Policy

Having worked on the international, national, state, and local levels on issues from creation care to fair wages to immigration to reproductive rights, houses of faith are no strangers to public policy advocacy that advances God's vision for the world. So it is with affordable housing. Even churches that never envisioned themselves attending city council meetings or walking the halls of state capitols have become savvy lobbyists to ensure that all neighbors are housed.

The Episcopal Church of the Advocate
in Chapel Hill: Small Church, Big Impact

After launching a new congregation and worshiping for eleven years in rented spaces, the people of the Episcopal Church of the Advocate in Chapel Hill, North Carolina, dreamed broadly and listened closely to their community. As home to the University of North Carolina at Chapel Hill—part of the booming Research Triangle Park economic hub and a popular destination for retirees—their city also showed signs of the national housing crisis. The quaint college town had its own set of haves and have-nots.

When the church acquired fifteen acres, it showed the foresight to list a range of possibilities for how it might use the land. It moved and restored an existing, modest, white, wood-frame chapel. It added office and gathering space. The congregation also included the possibility of housing in its special use permit, asking for an allowance of up to five thousand square feet of housing. The idea brought no attention in the routine public hearing to approve the land use, and the city approved the permit.

Church of the Advocate's example is noteworthy for several reasons. When the congregation mapped out its plans, it extended the infrastructure needed for its church buildings—electrical, water-sewer, plumbing, paving—to also serve housing located on space adjacent to the church buildings. It partnered with Pee Wee Homes to build three 350-square-foot tiny homes. They were to be independent, self-sufficient structures.

The total cost of the housing raised by Pee Wee Homes was $170,000, including related government development fees. Church of the Advocate contributed $2,000, and the Diocese of North Carolina another $10,000. The other funders were the town of Chapel Hill, grants, members of a graduate business school class at University of North Carolina, and individuals. In a city with upward-spiraling housing costs, the tiny homes provide safe and clean housing for people earning below 30 percent of the area median income. With incomes of between $700 and $1,100 per month, residents pay 30 percent of their income in rent. Pee Wee Homes saves some of the rental money to cover maintenance costs, and the rest funds an equity pool for the renters to use for housing when they move out.

These creative approaches were only part of the church's appetite for innovation and advocacy. Church leaders and Pee Wee Homes saw the need to work with town officials to explore the possibility of broadening local zoning ordinances and to encourage other church housing projects, says Rev. Lisa Fischbeck, who pastored Church of the Advocate at the time.

"Churches have property and infrastructure to keep costs down," she says. "Churches have a narrative that bids them to be involved and good souls ready and willing to help. But a town process can be arduous and discouraging, causing opportunities to be lost. The more we can streamline the process for churches to host affordable housing, the more affordable housing there will be."

Church of the Advocate's experience reflects the need for churches to engage with local public policy makers to advocate for ordinances that pave the way for more church-campus housing. Where they are underway, these efforts are most advanced where homelessness is most acute—and California is leading the way.

"Yes in God's Backyard" as Public Policy

In a hard-fought victory years in the making, advocates celebrated the adoption of California's SB 4 in 2023, otherwise known as the "Yes in God's Backyard" bill. The legislation grants houses of faith of all types permission to use their property to build affordable housing "by right," regardless of other local zoning restrictions. By opening up 171,000 acres of land on the campuses of churches and other houses of faith (along with college campuses), the bill aids developers of affordable housing who face difficulty in competing for affordable land with appropriate zoning.[7]

Illustrating the complexity of some public policy battles, the passage of the bill required an unusual agreement among several interested constituents, including environmentalists and labor and workplace safety interests. If only 25 percent of the land controlled by faith organizations were developed into affordable housing, the legislation could clear the way for hundreds of thousands of new affordable units in a range of desired neighborhoods. According to the Terner Center for Housing Innovation, by allowing development "by right," the legislation dramatically cuts down the current six- to eight-year average length of a church development project.[8]

Pastor John Oh told *Sojourners* in 2022 that he can list sixty-five congregations in the Los Angeles area alone that want to erect affordable units on their land. As the project manager for faith and housing at LA Voice, he sees the need for affordable housing on a daily basis—both from faith groups who want to make better use of their property, and from community members priced out of renting.

"Churches have been so amazing, helping people who are distressed," Oh said. "This is an opportunity for congregations to think about, 'How can we help with some of the root causes of the problem and not address it at the very end?'"[9]

Affordable housing advocates point out that the default zoning in most towns and cities anticipates single-family homes rather than allowing for more density and the potential for more housing at lower prices. That advantages existing neighbors who meet housing proposals with a response of "Not in my backyard" (NIMBY).

Churches and their advocacy partners have succeeded in changing public policy in multiple states and cities. Nadia Mian, senior program director of the Ralph W. Voorhees Center for Civic Engagement and a lecturer at the Edward J. Bloustein School of Planning and Public Policy at Rutgers University, and Rick Reinhard, principal of Niagara Consulting Group and associate at the Lakelands Institute in Montgomery County, Maryland, wrote this overview of public policy and related issues in the May 2023 issue of *Planning* magazine:

> In San Diego, Clairemont Lutheran Church was struggling to build affordable housing on its parking lot because parking requirements were tied to the linear amount of pews in the sanctuary. The church approached the city and an advocacy group, Yes in God's Backyard (YIGBY), for help. The collaboration paid off. In 2019, San Diego passed zoning reforms that reduce or remove parking requirements for redevelopment for affordable housing.
>
> "The parking requirement was really outdated for churches," says Brian Schoenfisch, deputy director of the City of San Diego's Department of Development Services, Urban Division. He notes that the regulations were created a half century ago when the city operated under "a very different model of suburban development." Planners worked with transportation and engineering staff to create a new formula.[10]

From there, the trend spread. The legislatures of California and Washington State and the cities of Pasadena and Seattle followed with their own policy changes in favor of faith-based affordable housing development.[11] The city governments of Atlanta and San Antonio launched initiatives that provide technical assistance and predevelopment grants, which often are a major obstacle to getting a project going. The Atlanta program aims to create two thousand units in collaboration with religious institutions.

These examples portend the years of work ahead in other areas of the country where the affordable housing crisis is not as pressing but is growing. In Charlotte, for example, the in-depth assessment of its housing challenge done by a team of 250 private, public, and non-profit sector leaders in 2021 overlooked possibilities for church land despite the initiative of the local churches documented here.

This might be explained by the scale of the housing gap in Charlotte and an assumption that the number of homes that can be built in partnership with houses of faith is relatively small and not worth the trouble. Some on Charlotte's city council, for example, emphasize the need for speed and scale in closing the housing gap. It also testifies to the power of the real estate industry in its local public policy advocacy and the bias of the marketplace to avoid the hard, low-profit-margin work of building affordable housing in creative ways.

I remain hopeful, however, that the vision, moral courage, creativity, and perseverance of the faith community will lead to the deeper inclusion of houses of faith in the solution to the housing crisis.[12]

The Role of Denominations and Ecumenical Networks

> The Church is to be a community of faith, entrusting itself to God alone, even at the risk of losing its life.
> *The Constitution of the Presbyterian Church (U.S.A.),*
> Part II, *Book of Order,* F-1.0301

In the early 2000s, the Charlotte Presbytery zigged when it could have zagged on a real estate matter. It paid a deep price. Elected presbytery leaders, lay and ordained, looked at the same growth projections used by real estate developers and put down a bet on the location of the next large church plant. For decades the city had spilled to the south and southeast of the center city, building suburb upon suburb that attracted mostly white families earning middle and upper incomes. Even as historic, urban Black Presbyterian churches struggled, the presbytery borrowed money and acquired a large tract in an affluent white suburb where it seemed the city's projected growth would warrant the next big church.

However, when the Great Recession of 2008 hit, real estate values plummeted. At the same time, congregations feeling their own financial pain began to cut what had been regular and in some cases generous financial support for the presbytery. Caught in a financial squeeze, the presbytery finally voted to cut its losses. In the end, the Charlotte Presbytery sold the land at a loss of $1 million. The budget impact forced the presbytery to slash its staff. In what is still one of the nation's largest presbyteries, the office started over with a bare minimum staff.

Now the winds have reversed. Since its close call with insolvency, the presbytery is watching its coffers grow—but for reasons that are

not the most welcomed. The wave of church closings that is coming for the nation has arrived in Charlotte, yielding a wealth of land
and financial assets totaling $7.3 million in just a few years. Proior
to 2024, the presbytery used some of the funds from property trans-
actions to add staff. It subsequently outlined a suggested allocation
model for the presbytery to follow to direct funds from property sales
and windfalls. One newly created fund from property transitions will
support the area's historic Black Presbyterian congregations, most of
which could not afford a full- or even part-time pastor. It also created
a fund where monies can be deposited for church renewal, revitalization, and experimentation.

Charlotte Presbytery's story represents what's happening nationwide. Judicatory bodies of all kinds are becoming stewards of hundreds of millions of dollars in land and buildings. In her two-year
study of the PC(USA)'s coming wave of property transfers, Rev.
Eileen Lindner reported that an estimated $100 million in Presbyte-
rian church property was sold in 2019, a figure that can be expected
to increase, perhaps dramatically, in the years to come.[13] In general,
denominational leaders are not well equipped, unto themselves, to
advise congregations about possibilities for their campuses in mission. Nor are they well positioned to manage their own growing real
estate and financial portfolios with courageous, missional imagination for the benefit of those in need of housing.

The success of the church housing movement thus far is a credit
to the courage, foresight, energy, innovation, perseverance, and generosity of individual churches. The stories captured here (and others
I didn't have room for) testify to each congregation's willingness to
find its way through the maze of questions and challenges that must
be navigated to complete a project. Denominational leaders face a
huge responsibility to help.

Church governance structures vary broadly. Some congregations
are islands unto themselves, free to determine their own property
uses. Those that belong to denominations such as the PC(USA) work
through connectional polity that gives voice and vote to churches
within the local denominational region. Some congregations have
the independence of owning their property. In most cases, however,
PC(USA) church property is ultimately owned by the presbytery

and thus is subject to its policies, polity, and processes and shared decision-making. Then there are congregations that are part of episcopate structures, including those in the United Methodist, Roman Catholic, and Episcopal Churches. They are bound by the decisions of district and diocesan councils and leaders with less autonomy or latitude at the congregational level.

With all the pressures facing local churches, national and regional denominational leaders have their hands full with many immediate challenges. As Christianity in America retracts (at least in the form of organized religion), denominational offices at the national and regional level are experiencing their own ongoing shake-ups and reorganizations. With these challenges and ever-shrinking operating budgets, there is little time and space for leaders to think several steps ahead.

For a variety of reasons, including trust and/or tendency to self-govern, local congregations can be wary about working with ecclesiastical offices. Yet denominations have increased their emphasis on innovation and experimentation at the local level. They are investing tens of millions of dollars to fund church revitalization and reimagination with some success. In initiatives such as the PC(USA)'s New Worshiping Communities and the United Methodist Church's Fresh Expressions, denominations are giving birth to new forms of church communities that are not rooted in buildings, land, and related expenses. These will create more nimble and responsive worshiping communities better suited for emerging church trends.

Denominations have also taken official positions on housing-related matters. The Episcopal Church, for example, has passed a range of national resolutions. One affirms housing "as a human right that should be provided for all individuals residing in the country." Another calls on governmental and diocese entities to "adequately fund housing assistance programs, and to address the ever-growing gap between affordable units and the number of renters in the bottom quartile of income."[14] As with its denominational siblings in the United States, however, the Episcopal Church has not appointed executive staff or resources to bring a strategic, holistic focus on the use of its land and buildings nationwide for the purposes of creating affordable housing.

Rev. Dr. Diane Moffett, president and executive director of the Presbyterian Mission Agency (a PC(USA) national office), sees the opportunity and says plainly, "Church buildings will become dinosaurs in many places in the next twenty to fifty years. . . . One day people will look back and talk about how churches used to build big buildings and gather and do everything there. The church has to realize what our faithfulness requires. How can our buildings become the center of ministry to bear witness to those on the margins, whose agency is limited by the grips of poverty? How can they be new centers of repair for historical harms?"

To equip more churches for the venture, Moffett said she favors a "both-and" approach to sharing know-how, technical skills, and lessons learned—"an exchange of learning from local presbyteries up and from the national office down." By hiring Corey Schlosser-Hall as deputy executive director for vision and innovation, Moffett has made building and sharing the expertise of the housing movement a national priority for the PC(USA). "We see this as a huge wave of the Holy Spirit which can both build the vitality of congregations *and* address the systemic injustice in the housing crisis while building community in neighborhoods around the country," Schlosser-Hall said.[15]

In the United Methodist Church, members of the Council of Bishops have discussed how to use land for housing. But the conversation has been more informal than formal. In a few regions of the United States, nonprofit developers have been created to dispense with church property or redevelop it. One of these, Wesley Community Development, was first chartered to handle real estate dispensation in western North Carolina and has since grown to operate across ten states in the eastern part of the country. A full-service real estate firm, Wesley Community Development has developed more than one thousand units of housing. President and CEO Joel Gilland says that church redevelopment is the fastest-growing part of the business: "Our goal is to help churches and denominations of all kinds through the disruption that is ahead in the next five years. If we are not careful, churches are going to transfer an awful lot of property to the private sector, and it's not coming back."

Where local congregations are taking their own initiative to build housing, their leaders say they are often educating their denominational staff leaders and superiors. In the leading edges of the movement in places like the mid-Atlantic and California, middle governing bodies have formed committees and collaboratives among congregations to share knowledge and best practices.

Given their stewardship responsibilities, denominations can do much more to assist local congregations with the pivotal decisions about their land and buildings that are sure to arise in the next ten to twenty years. Churches need assistance and encouragement in discernment, objective thinking about their futures, and a range of types of technical assistance. Steps are moving in that direction.

Where denominations have not yet stepped in, for-profit advisory firms and nonprofit organizations have formed networks of learning and advocacy. Rooted Good is an example, organized, in its words, "so faith-based organizations can align money and mission, reclaim their relevance in a changing world and be the church the world needs today."[16]

Having worked with a range of congregations, Mark Sampson of Rooted Good believes the need to share lessons learned will become increasingly important to help churches avoid lost time and costly mistakes. For example, he says, one church put months into pursuing a plan to build senior housing only to find there was no market demand for that type of housing in the church's area. An adviser would have recommended market research as a first step.

Collaboration is also needed when churches encounter neighborhood opposition and local zoning ordinances that make no room for housing on suburban church campuses. Wesley Community Development's Gilland says that denominations need to create databases to get their arms around how much property they control and to hire people with knowledge of real estate to coach local congregations.

"There is a scarcity mindset that many churches have, and it is driving decision-making to settle for the highest commercial payout possible," he says. "But we have to think about social impact rather than just how to make the most money. We all need to get much better to help churches navigate all that."

In Seattle, Oakland, and Washington, DC, among other places, Black churches are collaborating across denominational affiliation to grow the movement. They are building coalitions to work with city government and other organizations to advise churches as they advocate for housing and assess possibilities. As Nadia Mian wrote for *Shelterforce*, a publication devoted to affordable housing, "These efforts and initiatives are intended to soften the impact that gentrification and displacement have on low-income neighborhoods and communities of color as the cost of housing increases."[17]

In Los Angeles, the Faith Community Coalition acts as a network of pastors "to work with developers who are willing to enter into full partnerships with parishes, evenly splitting the revenues and paving the way for the houses of worship to eventually own the properties. So far, the alliance has more than 200 member churches, most of them African American."[18]

Still other entities provide resources, and there is growing attention from local governments. In Portland, Oregon, the city government published an extensive step-by-step guide for churches and houses of faith to follow in considering campus-based housing initiatives.[19]

Founded in the earliest years of the church housing movement, Enterprise Community Partners has developed hundreds of units of housing in the mid-Atlantic states, working primarily with Black churches. It is also working with the Wells Fargo Foundation in several cities. In Miami, for example, a $1.3-million fund would go toward helping fifteen South Florida congregations convert underused church property. In total, $8.5 million has been committed in a new push to help congregations in Atlanta, New York, Baltimore, Miami, and Seattle build affordable housing on their properties.

Preparing the Way: Bricks and Mortar PLUS Hearts and Minds

Every church-campus housing initiative involves a sea of facts, figures, bureaucracies, technical issues, public policy questions, congregational decisions, neighborhood conversations, and more. That's before construction begins. Then come the bricks and mortar, the wiring and plumbing, the furnishing and landscaping choices that create a place to live.

Creating a home, however, a space and place where true community can form, calls for education and preparation of a very different kind. In my research, I found that congregations often overlook the importance of preparing to meet and engage their new neighbors in appropriate ways. As with the foundation of a structure, the lack of proper preparation proves pivotal. Its absence can lead to cracks and faults in how church members and neighbors form healthy, respectful, and informed relationships, from move-in day and beyond.

In general, I found that congregations had not invested the time and energy needed for them to understand the hearts and minds, challenges and circumstances, and hopes and dreams of their on-campus neighbors. Of course, each neighbor is an individual child of God with distinct and personal needs and goals. Each must be met, known, loved, and cared for individually after moving in, at least to the degree they wish to be in relationship with church members. (At Caldwell, we remind ourselves that our primary mission is to house the unhoused and that, alone, spells success. Any relationship we make beyond that is a gift of grace.)

That doesn't mean congregations should wait for move-in day, show up with a casserole, and assume they will be fast friends with the resident. To the contrary, months of preparation are needed to help church members know how to be the best neighbors they can be. That preparation should be calibrated to the specific population that will live on campus, whether the neighbors are seniors, veterans, LGBTQ youth, working families, the chronically unhoused, or young adults who have aged out of foster care.

In the two years before our neighbors moved into Easter's Home at Caldwell, the congregation followed a rigorous "congregational preparation" curriculum to learn what we needed to know. Shaped by social workers, those with lived experience with homelessness, church members, and pastors, it offered a steady diet of various learning opportunities with the intent to engage as many church members as possible.

With an urban campus of only 1.3-acres, we know that our physical proximity to our neighbors living in Easter's Home will be close, at the very least.. We are creating an apartment building on a lot of the size that many single-family homes occupy. Twenty-one children of God will live on the same piece of land where church members and staff come and go every day and night. A range of community organizations meet and hold events in our Hope Hall space, which is dedicated to building community and offered at below-market rental rates. That means that almost daily, within 75 feet of Easter's Home, Hope Hall hosts children, adults, and those from across the city and from within our neighborhood.

A public elementary school neighbors the church on one side, and a medical office building on the other. Commercial businesses, restaurants, and offices animate one of the city's main thoroughfares a block away. The primary location of one of the city's two major hospitals sprawls across several nearby blocks. A streetcar carries commuters up and down the major thoroughfares that border Caldwell. Just behind the church, the city spent $6 million to update what was its first (and originally segregated) public park to attract families and events.

For all these reasons, we needed to know how best to receive and help our neighbors-to-be. More important, as those called to love our neighbors, we know they deserve to be treated with the dignity, respect, and care the world too often denies those on the margins. Some if not many will come with addictions and mental health challenges. We know their past pains and problems will, at times, create challenging scenarios and incidents. How those incidents are managed will define how we create community where all feel safe, known, heard, and seen. It's been said that 'community is built at the speed of trust.' So, how we handle moments when an Easter's Home neighbor may be in crisis can make or break their trust in us.

The Caldwell Congregational Preparation Team created the church's learning track by beginning with the values that rooted our mission. In the first three-month period, we focused on "dignity and empathy" along with "humility and lifelong learning." The next quarter we added "equity and racial justice," then "possibility and hope," then "proximity and community."

We read and discussed books, including *Shelter Theology: The Religious Lives of People without Homes* by Susan Dunlap, a chaplain to the unhoused, and *Grace Can Lead Us Home: A Christian Call to End Homelessness* by Kevin Nye, a pastor who worked with the chronically homeless in Los Angeles. Both authors led workshops at the church. As a majority white congregation, we deepened our study of antiracism and how attitudes of "white saviorism," conscious or not, can do harm.

We studied the principles and data behind the "housing first" approach. We invited specialists to teach us about trauma-informed care, harm reduction, mental health, first-aid training, and more. Pastors and leaders of churches elsewhere who had built housing shared their experiences, from the messy to the glorious. (See appendix D for a full outline of Caldwell's curriculum.)

As the experts suggested, a range of volunteers of all ages showed up to be "in proximity" with those who were unhoused—through serving meals and getting to know folks at shelters, volunteering at the service desk at the city's main day shelter, and other actions. We included those with lived experience as speakers in our events and workshops, each of which was attended by thirty to fifty members (out of about 350).

Several of our own members shared their experiences of being unhoused—times when their families slept in their cars or double-bunked with family or friends. One active leader who had discovered Caldwell as a guest in our homeless shelter kept us honest and humble along the way, reminding us of what we needed to know and learn. In the months immediately before our neighbors moved in, we shifted to role-playing to practice how to help our neighbors without enabling them, how to deescalate tricky situations, and more to ensure safety for all involved.

Caldwell members audited the neighborhood to identify the closest public transportation stops, grocery and drug stores, and other necessary services. We worked transparently and closely with the Elizabeth Community Association, which to its credit did not oppose the creation of Easter's Home. Whatever population a congregation welcomes to its campus housing, being prepared in these and many other ways will shape the relationships to be formed—good or bad, healthy or unhealthy, close or distant.

At Caldwell we were particularly blessed to have the guidance of member Lori Thomas, who holds both a master of divinity and a PhD in social work. An associate professor of social work at UNC Charlotte, she researches programmatic and systemic responses to homelessness and housing instability. (She also directs research at the UNC Charlotte Urban Institute and serves as the executive director of the Institute for Social Capital.) Time and again she helped

Caldwell hold its focus on finding the right service partner to create an atmosphere where our neighbors can succeed. She also reminds us regularly that our instincts to help, while well intended as followers of Christ, can backfire if we are not sensitive to the needs, lives, stories, and agency of our neighbors. She offered us this caution:

> The "housing first" model that we are implementing at Caldwell has extensive evidence supporting its effectiveness—both in keeping people off the streets and stabilizing lives. But unintentionally, operating out of a long faith tradition of helping, congregation members could also undermine what makes the model work. One example is how we will create space for our neighbors while leaving them choice and self-determination. Congregation members may be eager to fill up apartments and decorate rooms, but establishing your own decor and sense of place after not having housing may also be an important act of self-determination and control.

Developing awareness among church members about who they are and providing them the nuts and bolts of service and housing provision are important ways to prepare for new neighbors and to potentially create authentic communities not divided by labels of the helpers and the helped. (See appendix D for more details on learning resources.)

Building Belonging, Listening for Richard

I began this book asking whether koinonia—beloved community in God that gathers those of many different life stories, perspectives, experiences, ideas, and opinions—was still possible. It isn't easy, but the church has never been called to do easy things. Can we wade into this surely messy but healing and life-giving space? Can we see anew the God who created us in such splendid diversity, meant not to live apart but to grow together? Can we still be the beloved community that God in Christ came to usher in and commanded us to spread?

If you've read this far, you know that building housing on an active church campus is anything but the simplest way to create community. It is hard, just as with any important undertaking that changes lives, deepens our faith, reshapes even a corner of our cities, and reintroduces us to Christ in new ways. Every church I visited or researched tells tales of exhaustion, frustration, and the faith needed to take a risk without knowing precisely how it will turn out. Each in its own way knows, as Clarence Jordan said, that "faith is not belief in spite of the evidence but a life in scorn of the consequences."[20]

That stated, creating community and building belonging across differences can be truly transformational, even redemptive. The crisis of community that has befallen America has led to an epidemic of isolation. We are drowning in sadness, depression, a wave of suicides, and an epidemic of gun violence. We breathe antagonism and hide in our separate bubbles. We fail to seek the humanity in each other that can bridge our differences and ease our disagreements. We have retreated to our corners and are scared to come out. We have lost the courage, the confidence, and the faith to venture greatly.

Community is the prescription for what ails America. God makes us for community. America's separateness brings out the very worst in us. Life together, beyond our family or tribe, can bring out the very best of us, as planted in us by our Creator. Whether we live in good health, spiritual well-being, and material abundance or we don't know where we are going to sleep tonight, community heals us like nothing else.

For those on the streets, on the margins, or facing other daily challenges of living, data show that those who feel connected to others, who have some sense of belonging and purpose, live happier, healthier, and more stable lives. In fact, that is true for all of us. We feel better about ourselves and one another when we are bound together in a meaningful pursuit that calls out the best in us.

If America needs a great, shared cause to close the canyons that divide us, that is even more true for the church. This is keenly true now as the church stands at a historical crossroads. But it has always been true. The essence of the church, as the body of Christ, is not to fuel mere private pietism. The church is created to serve, to heal, to build, and to sustain us together, not alone, in community.

After years of living among and for the unhoused and others on the margins, author and pastor Kevin Nye puts it this way:

When the church is at its best, it celebrates community—what theologian Dietrich Bonhoeffer called "life together." Church buildings exist for the gathering of people. . . . Our most sacred tradition, the Lord's Supper, is known as "communion" because of the way it is practiced together. . . . The church is unique because everything it practices is done in community. . . .

We are created for relationships and communities; without these, we are incomplete. Disciples of Jesus are intended to be in communion with the poor, to be "always near." Our church communities are incomplete without solidarity with the poor and the marginalized in our neighborhoods. This communion resists social norms and upends economic division, enacting jubilee not as charity but as solidarity. When we can foster, come alongside and join in community with the unhoused, God is glorified, and we are all made more whole.[21]

Caldwell Presbyterian is scheduled to welcome our twenty-one new neighbors to Easter's Home in early 2025. We don't know their names yet, but we have been praying for them for years. We've also been praying that, with God's help, Easter's Home can live into its name as a place of recovery, renewal, rebirth, and, maybe in some small way, repair.

That prayer is as much for Caldwell members as it is for our neighbors-to-be. Living and interacting every day in close relationship on 1.3 acres with folks who have been on the streets for some length of time will be a calling unlike any we have ever answered. But our faith encourages us—and Richard Harrison goes ahead of us, with the Lord, to make a way.

Richard was to be our senior resident. He'd promised to set the tone for how Easter's Home would come into being as a place of community and belonging. We trusted Richard with that ministry for many reasons. Richard was a "churchman," and he thrived in that role. He loved church, and he made it better in such abundance that he contributed his presence and leadership to two active churches at once. He cherished his relationships at Myers Park United Methodist Church, a powerful, tall-steeple, affluent, white congregation where, as a Black man, he taught Sunday school, sang in the choir, led worship, and was a friend and adviser to its senior minister, Rev. Dr. James Howell.

There was so much of Richard that he had more to give—more love, more service, more faith, more witness, more testimony, and more hunger to experience church in a different context as well. He came to Caldwell for its commitment to social justice, passion for mission, intersectional diversity, and outward-facing welcome as a place where wounded souls can come to heal. He was elected as an elder and served with elegance, abiding wisdom, and deep spirituality.

We were always better when Richard was around, with his broad shoulders, square jaw, million-dollar smile, prayers "like Paul," and soulful singing voice that always hushed the room. It was a two-way relationship. At times, Richard needed church as a hospital for his soul, sometimes even two churches, because his life was not easy. He had integrated his high school in Ithaca, New York, and was uniquely called for that hard but groundbreaking work. He had an active mind, read voraciously, and tutored and mentored many young men. But as resilient as he was, something in him left when his son died.

Richard had a diagnosis that prevented him from working full-time. So he needed the permanent supportive housing with case management and other residential services that he and his neighbors received at McCreesh Place. We had counted on Richard to cut the ribbon and move into the first apartment at Easter's Home. The Lord, however, called him home in 2020.

But he is there in spirit to watch over the construction of the apartments, to inhabit the place spiritually, and to inspire us as we find our way in this great undertaking. Richard's spirit, I believe, also roams around. He was always most at home in a church. So he may be in your church's choir on Sunday morning. He may be listening in Sunday school or in the midst of your session or deacons meeting, quietly nudging, encouraging, maybe even nagging you a bit, to do the right thing as you strive to build the beloved community, however you do it, especially when it is hard.

If you would like to meet him, come visit Easter's Home any time. I am sure he will be nearby.

Appendix A

Index of the Initiatives
Researched for This Book

Appendix B

Principles of Discernment

The Importance of the How and the What
(Expanded from Chapter 3)

- Pray in everything! At the beginning and end of meetings, in the middle, in between and whenever needed, pray to hear the Spirit and lower the temperature of the discussion.
- Consider your church's history in its neighborhood or community. What elements of the church's past may be helpful to consider in the church's future?
- Define a pathway for the process the congregation will follow, including labeling as many steps as possible, on the front end. Help members understand that it is a journey, not one or two meetings and then a predetermined destination. Show everyone interested or involved in the process a road map—graphically if you can, like a game board, highlighting each step as it is taken.
- Communicate, communicate, communicate. Then communicate some more. Be transparent in everything. People will naturally wonder whether some voices are being heard over others, whether their input is being heard, and whether you are following the path you set out. To build trust and buy-in, address those questions repeatedly along the way, even before they are asked.
- Try to identify what you don't know, and bring in experts. Whatever breaks God's heart in your community, whatever issue you feel called to consider, you probably don't have all the expertise and perspective in your congregation to know what you need to know.

- Listen more than talk, especially in the first stages of discernment. Sometimes we don't do that as well as we might, especially if we are passionate and convicted about what *we* think God is up to.
- If you expect those with strong, perhaps previously expressed ideas and opinions to engage, take the first step to ensure they know their input will be heard, recorded, and shared with all. Be equitable with their input without special treatment.
- Make it clear that the widow who gives her mite is as valued as the matriarch or patriarch who furnished the parlor or bought the new sanctuary carpet.
- Model grace, and ask for it from all—but know that it won't always show up. To create places for candor and safety in expressing all ideas, perspectives, and emotions, set ground rules for meetings up front, and review them as many times as it takes.
- Center the voice of the other, the newcomer, the outsider to make it clear that the process is a level playing field. Consider resources that ground the group in the ways of antiracism and avoidance of microaggressions. Seek first to do no harm. Once someone pulls away from the process because they feel slighted, it can be very hard to reengage them.
- Use a diverse and representative set of leaders in facilitating these meetings, giving them a little coaching or training as needed. *Don't* depend on your pastor or other staff to lead everything. Help them take a back seat when needed.
- If you can, recruit a third-party facilitator, paid or unpaid, to be your pilot—someone who can ensure neutrality and fairness.
- And pray without ceasing!

Sources of Construction and Development Funding for Easter's Home

This list shows the sources of construction and development funding for Easter's Home, an adaptive building reuse initiative sponsored by Caldwell Presbyterian Church in Charlotte, North Carolina, that provides housing and supportive services for those who have experienced chronic homelessness.

Caldwell Presbyterian Capital Campaign	$800,000
Myers Park United Methodist Grant	$1,000,000
North Carolina Housing Finance Agency	$600,000
Merancas Foundation Grant	$500,000
City of Charlotte Housing Trust Fund Grant	$630,000
American Rescue Plan Act Grant through Mecklenburg County	$2,500,000
Total	$6,030,000

Caldwell Presbyterian Church's Curriculum for Preparation

Here are the resources that made up Caldwell Presbyterian's "curriculum" of study to prepare church members to be neighbors to the residents of Easter's Home.

Easter's Coming: Toward The Beloved Community

Join the Caldwell community as we spend 2023 and 2024 moving toward the beloved community by getting ready for Easter's Home. We will offer different ways to learn—reading, workshops, panels, learning from people with lived experience, and getting out in the community to be proximate/nearer to our neighbors.

Congregational Preparation Objectives

1. Acknowledge and explore our deeply held and socially conditioned assumptions about people experiencing homelessness and deep poverty.
2. Acknowledge and explore proximity, community, and our deeply held assumptions about helping.
3. Increase our understanding of homelessness, housing first, and the organizations/systems that address housing instability and deep poverty in our community.

4. Prepare and practice for challenges that will arise so that we respond as beloved community rather than react from stereotypical assumptions.
5. Create tools, skills, and practices that help us live into our values.
6. Cultivate our own openness to change and possibility.

Working Values Guiding Our Preparation
- Dignity/empathy
- Equity/racial justice
- Humility/lifelong learning
- Possibility/hope
- Proximity/community

Our Timeline/Syllabus
January–March 2023: Understanding Homelessness
- Guiding values: dignity/empathy; humility/lifelong learning
- Reading: *Shelter Theology* by Susan Dunlap
- Workshops/learnings
- Presentation and dialogue with Susan Dunlap, author of *Shelter Theology*
- Homelessness and Housing 101
- Proximity/community action: serve breakfast at the Urban Ministry Center

April–June 2023: Understanding Ourselves
- Guiding values: humility/lifelong learning; equity/racial justice
- Reading: *Grace Can Lead Us Home* by Kevin Nye
- Workshops/learnings
- Antiracism and the Black History of Charlotte/Mecklenburg County
- Rev. Krista Fregoso, St. Paul's Episcopal (Walnut Creek, California), shared preaching/dialogue
- Proximity/community action: serve dinner at Roof Above's Howard Levine Shelter

July–September 2023: Understanding Housing First
- Guiding values: humility/lifelong learning; possibility/hope
- Reading: *Grace Can Lead Us Home* by Kevin Nye
- Workshops/learnings
- Antiracism and the risk of "white saviorism"
- Workshop with Kevin Nye
- Proximity/community action: serve dinner at Roof Above's Howard Levine Shelter

October–December 2023: Building Skills and Tools
- Guiding values: dignity/empathy; proximity/community
- Workshops/panels
- Case management discussion: ACE Sunday school class
- Webinar with Sam Tsemberis, founder of Housing First

Diving Deeper to Understand the Lives of Our Neighbors: 2024
April
    Housing First University: three-hour virtual training on permanent supportive housing

May
    Housing First University: introduction to harm reduction and proximate service

June
    Project update and Q&A town hall

July
    Poverty simulation and panel of People with Lived Experience in Poverty

September
    Learning event with Easter's Home's Lived Experience Advisory Panel

October
    Workshop for churches on building housing
    Monthly proximate service

November
> Presbytery-wide one-day workshop on churches building housing
> Anti-racism workshop
> Trauma-informed care workshop
> Monthly proximate service

December
> Monthly proximate service

January
> Workshops with Kevin Adler, coauthor of *When We Walk By: Forgotten Humanity, Broken Systems, and the Role We Can Each Play in Ending Homelessness in America*
> "What to Do When . . .": role-playing training to know how to best support our new neighbors as they settle in
> Monthly proximate service

February
> Meet the staff of Easter's Home
> "What to Do When . . .": role-playing training to know how to best support our new neighbors as they settle in
> Monthly proximate service

March
> Tour of Easter's Home
> Monthly proximate service

April
> Grand opening of Easter's Home
> Neighbors move in

Other Tools and Resources
- Caldwell has created an online library of recorded workshops and other educational sessions related to housing and homelessness (https://www.caldwellpresby.org/easter/) for members and others to access. The church will repeat key workshops and supplement its resources as new members and partners join the church

and/or volunteer with Easter's Home. We know our learning will be ongoing, and we intend to share it.

- Prior to our neighbors moving in, the church will create a committee focused on extending hospitality and building beloved community with residents.

Notes

Chapter 1: Making God's House a Home

1. "What Is Area Median Income (AMI)?" Janover HUD Loans, updated June 5, 2023, https://www.hud.loans/hud-loans-blog/what-is-area-median-income-ami.
2. "Housing and Neighborhood Services 2023, Area Median Family Income Charlotte, NC, HouseCharlotte Program AMI Matrix—Effective June 15, 2023," https://dreamkeypartners.org/wp-content/uploads/2023/06/AMI-Affordability-Income-Limits-June-15-2023-House-Charlotte.pdf.
3. "State of Homelessness: 2023 Edition," National Alliance to End Homelessness, https://endhomelessness.org/homelessness-in-america/homelessness-statistics/state-of-homelessness.
4. *Cambridge Dictionary*, s.v. "crisis (n.)," https://dictionary.cambridge.org/us/dictionary/english/crisis.
5. Sonali Mathur, "Are Renters and Homeowners in Rural Areas Cost Burdened?" *Housing Perspectives*, Joint Center for Housing Studies of Harvard University, August 11, 2016, https://www.jchs.harvard.edu/blog/are-renters-and-homeowners-in-rural-areas-cost-burdened#:~:text=Indeed%2C%20fully%2041%20percent%20of,of%20their%20income%20on%20housing.
6. "How Much Do You Need to Earn to Afford a Modest Apartment in Your State?" National Low Income Housing Coalition, https://nlihc.org/oor.
7. *Cambridge Dictionary*, s. v. "crisis (n.)"
8. Richard Reinhard, "Redeveloping Houses of Worship," ICMA, April 1, 2021, https://icma.org/articles/pm-magazine/redeveloping-houses-worship.
9. Mark Elsdon, *Gone for Good: Negotiating the Coming Wave of Church Property Transition* (Grand Rapids: Eerdmans, 2024), 32.

167

10. National Low Income Housing Coalition, "The Gap: A Shortage of Affordable Homes, April 2022, https://nlihc.org/sites/default/files/gap/Gap-Report _2022.pdf.
11. William Brosend, "The People's Preaching Class: Fred Craddock in Retirement," *The Christian Century*, March 4, 2015, https://www.christiancentury .org/article/2015-02/people-s-preaching-class.

Chapter 2: God's Ideas about Land, Shelter, and Economy

1. Walter Brueggemann, *The Land: Place as Gift, Promise, and Challenge in Biblical Faith* (Minneapolis: Augsburg Fortress, 2002), 43.
2. Brueggemann, 61.
3. Brueggemann, 62, 55, 52; Scripture reference is from the Revised Standard Version.
4. M. Douglas Meeks, *God the Economist: The Doctrine of God and Political Economy* (Minneapolis: Fortress Press, 1989), 111.
5. Shane Claiborne, *The Irresistible Revolution: Living as an Ordinary Radical* (Grand Rapids: Zondervan, 2006), 194.
6. Julie Zauzmer, "Christians Are More Than Twice as Likely to Blame a Person's Poverty on Lack of Effort," *Washington Post*, August 3, 2017, https:// www.washingtonpost.com/news/acts-of-faith/wp/2017/08/03/christians-are -more-than-twice-as-likely-to-blame-a-persons-poverty-on-lack-of-effort.
7. William Stringfellow, *A Public and Private Faith* (Grand Rapids: Eerdmans, 1965), 95.
8. Clarence Jordan, *The Substance of Faith, and Other Cotton Patch Sermons* (Eugene, OR: Wipf and Stock, 2005), 43.

Chapter 3: The Church at the Convergence

1. Phyllis Tickle, *The Great Emergence: How Christianity Is Changing and Why* (Grand Rapids: Baker Books, 2012), 16. Tickle cites the Right Reverend Mark Dyer, an Anglican bishop, as the one who observed the five-hundred-year rummage sale in church history.
2. *The Constitution of the Presbyterian Church (U.S.A.)*, Part II: *Book of Order* (Louisville, KY: Office of the General Assembly, Presbyterian Church (U.S.A.), 2019–2023), F-1.0304.
3. Katherine Schaeffer, "Key Facts about Housing Affordability in the U.S.," Pew Research Center, March 23, 2022, https://www.pewresearch.org/short -reads/2022/03/23/key-facts-about-housing-affordability-in-the-u-s.
4. "How Much Do You Need to Earn to Afford a Modest Apartment in Your State?" National Low Income Housing Coalition, https://nlihc.org/oor.
5. "How Much Do You Need to Earn?"
6. "The Problem," National Low Income Housing Coalition, https://nlihc.org /explore-issues/why-we-care/problem#:~:text=Nationally%2C%20there%20 is%20a%20shortage,plus%20extremely%20low%2Dincome%20families.

7. Patrick Sisson, "Affordable Housing Woes Paint a 'Bleak Picture,'" *New York Times*, June 14, 2023, https://www.nytimes.com/2023/06/14/business/affordable-housing-developers.html.

8. U.S. Interagency Council on Homelessness, "Fiscal Year 2019 Performance and Accountability Report, November 2018, https://www.usich.gov/sites/default/files/document/FY2019_USICH_PAR_FINAL.pdf.

9. "Housing First Works: Report Sheds Light on Program to End Homelessness," UNC Charlotte Urban Institute, November 12, 2020, https://ui.charlotte.edu/story/housing-first-works-report-sheds-light-program-end-homelessness.

10. CSH, "FAQs about Supportive Housing Research: Is Supportive Housing Cost Effective?" https://www.csh.org/wp-content/uploads/2018/06/Cost-Effectiveness-FAQ.pdf.

11. Schaeffer, "Key Facts about Housing Affordability."

12. I am grateful to Jill Suzanne Shook and her coauthors' brief history of housing in *Making Housing Happen: Faith-Based Affordable Housing Models* (Eugene, OR: Cascade Books, 2012).

13. Robert Wuthnow, *Faith Communities and the Fight for Racial Justice: What Has Worked, What Hasn't, and Lessons We Can Learn* (Princeton, NJ: Princeton University Press, 2023), 40.

14. "The State of the Nation's Housing 2022," Joint Center for Housing Studies of Harvard University, https://www.jchs.harvard.edu/sites/default/files/reports/files/Harvard_JCHS_State_Nations_Housing_2022.pdf.

15. Sophie Kasakove and Robert Gebeloff, "The Shrinking of the Middle-Class Neighborhood," *New York Times*, July 6, 2022, https://www.nytimes.com/2022/07/06/us/economic-segregation-income.html?smid=nytcore-ios-share&referringSource=articleShare.

16. Jerusalem Demsas, "The Obvious Answer to Homelessness, *Atlantic*, January/February 2023, https://www.theatlantic.com/magazine/archive/2023/01/homelessness-affordable-housing-crisis-democrats-causes/672224.

17. "The Shrinking of the Middle-Class Neighborhood," https://www.nytimes.com/2022/07/06/us/economic-segregation-income.html?.

18. Elizabeth Kneebone, "The Changing Geography of U.S. Poverty," Brookings, February 15, 2017, https://www.brookings.edu/testimonies/the-changing-geography-of-us-poverty.

19. "The Gap: A Shortage of Affordable Homes," National Low Income Housing Coalition, April 2022, https://nlihc.org/sites/default/files/gap/Gap-Report_2022.pdf.

20. Saint Ireneaus, *Against Heresies*, https://ia804501.us.archive.org/11/items/SaintIrenaeusAgainstHeresiesComplete/Saint%20Irenaeus%20Against%20Heresies%20Complete.pdf, 235.

21. Martin Luther King Jr., *Where Do We Go from Here: Chaos or Community?* (New York: Harper & Row, 1967), 161.

22. King, 196–97.

23. Peter Block, *Community: The Structure of Belonging* (Oakland, CA: Berrett-Koehler, 2018), xviii.

24. *Thayer's Greek–English Lexicon of the New Testament*, 4th ed., s.v. "koinonia."

25. Eric D. Barreto, "Belonging," interview with Willie James Jennings, *Presbyterian Outlook*, updated April 5, 2023, https://pres-outlook.org/2023/03/belonging.

26. "Religion," Gallup, https://news.gallup.com/poll/1690/Religion.aspx.

27. Jeffrey M. Jones, "Church Attendance Has Declined in Most U.S. Religious Groups," Gallup, March 25, 2024, https://news.gallup.com/poll/642548/church-attendance-declined-religious-groups.aspx.

28. Jones, "Church Attendance Has Declined in Most U.S. Religious Groups."

29. Greg Brekke, "Feeling the Squeeze: Financial Pressures Add Up for PC(USA) Congregations," *Presbyterian Outlook*, updated March 11, 2024, https://pres-outlook.org/2023/12/feeling-the-squeeze-financial-pressures-add-up-for-pcusa-congregations.

30. "Twenty Years of Congregational Change: The 2020 Faith Communities Today Overview," https://faithcommunitiestoday.org/wp-content/uploads/2021/10/Faith-Communities-Today-2020-Summary-Report.pdf.

31. Richard Reinhard, "Redeveloping Houses of Worship," ICMA, April 1, 2021, https://icma.org/articles/pm-magazine/redeveloping-houses-worship.

32. Block, *Community*, 49.

33. Lenny Duncan, *Dear Church: A Love Letter from a Black Preacher to the Whitest Denomination in the U.S.* (Minneapolis: Fortress Press, 2019), 124.

34. Duncan, 147.

35. Duncan, 127.

36. *Book of Order*, F-1.0404.

37. Initially, Caldwell Presbyterian had played an instrumental role in planting Seigle Avenue Presbyterian, with the intent to build a church where new public housing had been built after World War II. In time, residents of the public housing and of the surrounding neighborhood shifted from white to Black. Drug dealers moved in and preyed on the poor, bringing crime and violence. Seigle Avenue, however, remained planted. Offering regular, open church dinners and children's programming every Wednesday and an equally open worship environment on Sundays, relationships between the members and the families in the area grew.

38. For more details on the story of Caldwell and the resurrecting of other diverse, missional PC(USA) churches like Caldwell, see John Cleghorn, *Resurrecting Church: Where Justice and Diversity Meet Radical Welcome and Healing Hope* (Minneapolis: Fortress Press, 2021).

39. This building was named in honor of W. E. Price, a Caldwell elder and moderator of the Presbyterian Church in the United States in 1949.

Chapter 4: One City's Confluence

1. United States Census Bureau, "Large Southern Cities Lead Nation in Population Growth," press release no. CB23-79, May 18, 2023, https://www.census.gov /newsroom/press-releases/2023/subcounty-metro-micro-estimates.html?utm _source=newsletter&utm_medium=email&utm_campaign=newsletter_axios am&stream=top.

2. Chase Jordan, "Million-Dollar Homes in the Charlotte Region Are on the Rise, Following National Trend," *Charlotte Observer*, updated September 11, 2023, https://www.charlotteobserver.com/news/business /article278983139.html?ac_cid=DM846226&ac_bid=-356554749; Mary Ann Priester and Jessica Lefkowitz, "Bridging the Gap: Addressing Unsheltered Homelessness in Charlotte-Mecklenburg," Charlotte-Mecklenburg Housing and Homelessness Dashboard, https://mecklenburghousingdata .org/frontpage-article/bridging-the-gap-addressing-unsheltered-homeless ness-in-charlotte-mecklenburg.

3. Tom Hanchett, *Sorting Out the New South City: Race, Class, and Urban Development in Charlotte, 1875–1975* (Chapel Hill: University of North Carolina Press, 1998), 3.

4. Some claim that the locally well-known Mecklenburg Declaration even preceded the nation's Declaration of Independence.

5. Jim Crow laws were a collection of state and local statutes that legalized racial segregation.

6. Hanchett, *Sorting Out the New South City*, 119.

7. Hanchett, 151.

8. For more, see Danyelle Solomon, Connor Maxwell, and Abril Castro, "Systemic Inequality: Displacement, Exclusion, and Segregation," Center for American Progress, August 7, 2019, https://www.americanprogress.org/article /systemic-inequality-displacement-exclusion-segregation. Also see Richard Rothstein, *The Color of Law: A Forgotten History of How Our Government Segregated America* (New York: Liveright, 2017).

9. This history is recounted in many places, including "History of the Brooklyn Community," an article on the website of the J. Murray Atkins Library at the University of North Carolina at Charlotte (https://guides.library.charlotte .edu/c.php?g=621704&p=4626874). Author Greg Jarrell offers a powerful look at Brooklyn's demise and the role of white supremacy in *Our Trespasses: White Churches and the Taking of American Neighborhoods* (Minneapolis: Fortress Press, 2024).

10. Jarrell, *Our Trespasses*, 3.

11. "Urban Redevelopment," Encyclopedia.com, updated June 8, 2018, https:// www.encyclopedia.com/history/united-states-and-canada/us-history/urban -renewal.

12. Alexandria Sands, "The Latest on the Long-Delayed, Much-Anticipated Brooklyn Redevelopment," Axios Charlotte, February 26, 2024, https://

www.axios.com/local/charlotte/2024/02/26/brooklyn-village-construction
-development?utm_source=newsletter&utm_medium=email&utm_campaign
=newsletter_axioslocal_charlotte&stream=top.

13. "Elizabeth, Charlotte, NC," realtor.com, https://www.realtor.com/realestate
andhomes-search/Elizabeth_Charlotte_NC/overview. My family owned a
home in Elizabeth for fifteen years.

14. Charlotte/Mecklenburg Quality of Life Explorer, https://mcmap.org
/qol/#15.

15. "Addressing the Opportunity Gap for Charlotte's Children," UNC Charlotte
Urban Institute, May 14, 2015, https://ui.charlotte.edu/story/addressing
-opportunity-gap-charlotte%E2%80%99s-children.

16. Raj Chetty, Nathaniel Hendren, Patrick Kline, and Emmanuel Saez, "Where
Is the Land of Opportunity? The Geography of Intergenerational Mobility
in the United States," June 2014, https://scholar.harvard.edu/files/hendren
/files/mobility_geo.pdf.

17. Alana Semuels, "Why It's So Hard to Get Ahead in the South," *Atlantic*,
April 4, 2017, https://www.theatlantic.com/business/archive/2017/04/south
-mobility-charlotte/521763.

18. "Housing First," National Alliance to End Homelessness, March 20, 2022,
https://endhomelessness.org/resource/housing-first.

19. Jennifer Ludden, "'It Is the Obvious Thing': The White House Tries a New
Tack to Combat Homelessness," NPR.com, December 19, 2022, https://
www.npr.org/2022/12/19/1142790156/people-homelessness-crisis-housing
-prevention-biden.

20. Chyna Blackmon, "Charlotte's Current Rent Outpaces National Average in
2023," *Charlotte Observer*, March 21, 2023, https://www.charlotteobserver.com
/news/local/know-your-704/article273413120.html?ac_cid=DM777399&ac
_bid=-1847721510.

21. Charlotte-Mecklenburg Housing and Homelessness Data Factsheet 2021, https://
secureservercdn.net/166.62.110.60/z4b.66d.myftpupload.com/wp-content
/uploads/2021/10/2021-Charlotte-Mecklenburg-Housing-Data-Factsheet.pdf.

22. Anthony Gardner, "The Rent Report, March 2024," https://www.rent.com
/research/average-rent-price-report.

23. The trend wasn't limited to Hidden Valley. By 2023, corporate landlords
owned about 12 percent of all homes in Mecklenburg County. In Charlotte,
some corporate landlords even built entire new-home subdivisions filled only
with for-rent and by-the-bedroom houses. About two dozen large, national corporations owned more than forty thousand single-family homes across North
Carolina, largely concentrated in the state's urban centers.
   Opinions of this approach to rental housing vary. Proponents say it provides an additional way for renters to find affordable living space. Others com-
plain that these investment groups purchase existing affordable properties only
to drive up the costs. Analysts estimate that the groups have shifted billions

of dollars in local homeownership out of local hands. They also question the long-term viability of the investment model and wait for the consequences of an exodus of investors when the real estate market softens.

24. D. J. Simmons, "Black Homeownership Is Hidden Valley's Legacy; Now Corporate Landlords Threaten That," *Charlotte Observer*, February 7, 2023, https://www.charlotteobserver.com/news/local/article270738587.html?ac_cid=DM 753034&ac_bid=1919405547.

25. Lisa Vernon Sparks, "Steadfast in Its Mission, Charlotte Habitat for Humanity Battles Rising Home Prices," *Charlotte Observer*, December 8, 2023, https://www.charlotteobserver.com/article279933779.html.

26. "Charlotte's Greater Bethel AME Church to Sell Land to Habitat Charlotte Region for Construction of Affordable Housing Community," Habitat for Humanity of the Charlotte Region, November 2, 2021, https://www.habitat cltregion.org/news/charlottes-greater-bethel-ame-church-to-sell-land-to-habitat -charlotte-region-for-construction-of-affordable-housing-community.

27. "Chronically Homeless," National Alliance to End Homelessness, updated December 2023, https://endhomelessness.org/homelessness-in-america/who -experiences-homelessness/chronically-homeless/#:~:text=People%20who% 20are%20chronically%20homeless,Updated%20April%202023.

28. "A Home for All," United Way of Greater Charlotte, https://unitedwaygreater clt.org/a-home-for-all/.

29. "A Home for All."

Chapter 5: The Faces of the Movement

1. Phyllis Tickle, *The Great Emergence: How Christianity Is Changing and Why* (Grand Rapids: Baker Books, 2012).

2. Martin Luther King Jr., *Where Do We Go from Here: Chaos or Community?* (New York: Harper & Row, 1967), 6.

3. Jill Suzanne Shook, *Making Housing Happen: Faith-Based Affordable Housing Models* (Eugene, OR: Cascade Books, 2012), 276.

4. "Abyssinian Development Corporation, New York," OECD iLibrary, https://read.oecd-ilibrary.org/urban-rural-and-regional-development/organising-local -economic-development/abyssinian-development-corporation-new-york_9789 264083530-12-en#page7.

5. Elliott Wright, *Partnerships Spark Revitalized Neighborhoods*, Progressions: A Lilly Endowment Occasional Report (Indianapolis: Lilly Endowment, 1996).

6. Wright, *Partnerships Spark Revitalized Neighborhoods.*

7. For an excellent in-depth overview of CDCs and faith coalitions, see Robert Wuthnow, *Faith Communities and the Fight for Racial Justice: What Has Worked, What Hasn't, and Lessons We Can Learn* (Princeton, NJ: Princeton University Press, 2023).

8. Andy Marzo and Daniel Stevens, AICP, "Humanizing Data: Area Median Income (AMI) and Affordable Housing Policy," Camoin Associates, March 13,

2023, https://camoinassociates.com/resources/humanizing-data-area-median
-income-ami-and-affordable-housing-policy.

9. Gregg Colburn and Page Alder Clayton, *Homelessness Is a Housing Problem: How Structural Factors Explain U.S. Patterns* (Berkeley: University of California Press, 2022).
10. David Garcia, Quinn Underriner, Muhammad Alameldin, and Issi Romem, "The Housing Potential for Land Owned by Faith-Based Organizations and Colleges," Terner Center for Housing Innovation, August 2023, https://ternercenter.berkeley.edu/wp-content/uploads/2023/08/Faith-Based-Housing-Updated-October-2023.pdf.
11. "Our Story," Clarendon Baptist Church, https://www.1bc.org/our-story.
12. Marty Haugen, "All Are Welcome," *Glory to God: The Presbyterian Hymnal* (Louisville, KY: Westminster John Knox Press, 2013), #301.
13. U.S. Department of Housing and Urban Development, https://www.hudexchange.info.
14. "Affordable Housing Initiative," Fairfax Presbyterian Church, https://fairfaxpresbyterian.org/fpc/affordable-housing.
15. Shawna Bowman, "Merged Congregations Addressing Racism, Hatred, Housing," *Presbyterian Outlook*, updated May 16, 2023, https://pres-outlook.org/2023/05/innovators-in-ministry-you-should-know.
16. Bowman, "Merged Congregations Addressing Racism, Hatred, Housing."
17. Arlington Partnership for Affordable Housing, "Central United Methodist Church and Arlington Partnership for Affordable Housing Break Ground on Ballston Redevelopment," press release, December 9, 2021, https://apah.org/central-united-methodist-church-and-arlington-partnership-for-affordable-housing-break-ground-on-ballston-redevelopment.
18. Thom S. Rainer, "Ten Major Trends for Local Churches in America in 2023," Church Answers, December 26, 2022, https://churchanswers.com/blog/ten-major-trends-for-local-churches-in-america-in-2023/.
19. "Wesley Housing Opens the Waypoint at Fairlington—Alexandria's Newest Affordable Multifamily Community," Wesley Housing, September 29, 2022, https://wesleyhousing.org/wesley-housing-opens-the-waypoint-at-fairlington-alexandrias-newest-affordable-multifamily-community.
20. I am grateful to Rev. Lisa Fischbeck for her research behind these five stories, which was made possible through a grant awarded her by Louisville Institute to find and tell the stories of what small and rural churches are doing in the affordable housing movement.

Chapter 6: Board by Board, Brick by Brick, Home by Home

1. "NLIHC Releases *Out of Reach 2023: The High Cost of Housing*," June 14, 2023, National Low Income Housing Coalition, https://nlihc.org/resource/nlihc-releases-out-reach-2023-high-cost-housing.
2. Walter Brueggemann, *The Land: Place as Gift, Promise, and Challenge in Biblical Faith* (Minneapolis: Augsburg Fortress, 2002), 56, 57–58.

3. Robert Wuthnow, *Faith Communities and the Fight for Racial Justice: What Has Worked, What Hasn't, and Lessons We Can Learn* (Princeton, NJ: Princeton University Press, 2023), 72.
4. Wuthnow, 72.
5. Kevin Nye, *Grace Can Lead Us Home: A Christian Call to End Homelessness* (Harrisonburg, VA: Herald Press, 2022), 23.
6. From an Enterprise Community Partners panel on churches building housing, 2022.
7. Scott Wiener, "Senator Wiener's YIGBY—Yes in God's Backyard—Bill Passes the Assembly," press release, September 7, 2023, https://sd11.senate.ca.gov/news/senator-wieners-yigby-yes-gods-backyard-bill-passes-assembly.
8. David Garcia, Quinn Underriner, Muhammad Alameldin, and Issi Romem, "The Housing Potential for Land Owned by Faith-Based Organizations and Colleges," Terner Center for Housing Innovation, August 2023, https://ternercenter.berkeley.edu/wp-content/uploads/2023/08/Faith-Based-Housing-Updated-October-2023.pdf.
9. Julia Oller, "Will California Churches Build Affordable Housing 'in God's Backyard'?" *Sojourners*, July 7, 2022, https://sojo.net/articles/will-california-churches-build-affordable-housing-god-s-backyard.
10. Nadia Mian and Richard T. Reinhard, "Transforming Empty Churches into Affordable Housing Takes More Than a Leap of Faith," *Planning*, May 5, 2023, https://www.planning.org/planning/2023/spring/transforming-empty-churches-into-affordable-housing-takes-more-than-a-leap-of-faith.
11. California followed San Diego's lead in 2020 when it passed AB1851, legislation that reduces or eliminates parking requirements for faith-based affordable housing developments. In Pasadena, the zoning ordinance was changed to permit religious institutions in certain areas of the city to build up to thirty-six affordable dwelling units per acre. Washington State adopted into law HB1377 in 2019, allowing municipalities to provide a density bonus for housing on church-owned properties as long as it is affordable to those making up to 80 percent of the area median income and remains affordable for fifty years. Seattle adopted the legislation in 2021 after holding public outreach sessions, but it deepened the affordability requirement to 60 percent of area median income—and won the Governor's Smart Housing Strategies Award for its work.
12. In 2023 and early 2024, Charlotte Mayor Vi Lyles and the city council increased their focus on working with faith communities.
13. Mark Elsdon, *Gone for Good: Negotiating the Coming Wave of Church Property Transition* (Grand Rapids: Eerdmans, 2024), 28.
14. "Policy for Action: An Index of Episcopal Church Public Policy Resolutions," Office of Government Relations of the Episcopal Church, 2023, https://www.episcopalchurch.org/wp-content/uploads/sites/2/2023/07/Policy-for-Action-OGR-2023.pdf, 49.

15. Cory Schlosser-Hall (Deputy Executive Director for Vision and Innovation, Presbyterian Mission Agency, Presbyterian Church (U.S.A.), in an interview with the author, July 31, 2023. Within and beyond denominational structures, a growing focus on "church redevelopment" is helping congregations consider the best and highest use of their property, which shouldn't always mean the highest monetary payoff. The Presbyterian Foundation, for example, launched Project Regeneration to encourage congregations to think ahead about the use of their property, whether the church forecasts closing or is looking for new mission ideas. For more information, visit https://www.presbyterianfoundation.org/project-regeneration/.

16. "About Us," Rooted Good, https://www.rootedgood.org/about-us.

17. Nadia Mian, "Black Congregations Are Developing Housing on Church Land," *Shelterforce*, January 17, 2023, https://shelterforce.org/2023/01/17/black-churches-become-affordable-housing-developers. See also Elsdon, *Gone for Good*, which is an excellent resource on church property possibilities.

18. Religion News Service, "In Southern California, Black Churches Are Using Their Land to Build Housing for Homeless People," *Presbyterian Outlook*, March 17, 2021, https://pres-outlook.org/2021/03/in-southern-california-black-churches-are-using-their-land-to-build-housing-for-homeless-people.

19. "Religious Institutions and Affordable Housing Development Projects," https://www.portland.gov/bds/religious-institutions-and-affordable-housing-development-projects.

20. Clarence Jordan, *The Substance of Faith, and Other Cotton Patch Sermons* (Eugene, OR: Wipf and Stock, 2005), 43.

21. Kevin Nye, *Grace Can Lead Us Home: A Christian Call to End Homelessness* (Harrisonburg, VA: Herald Press, 2022), 103.